D1487394

DOES SUFFERING MAKE SENSE?

DOES SUFFERING MAKE SENSE?

RUSSELL SHAW

SCEPTER PUBLISHERS
Princeton, New Jersey

Scripture quotations in this work are from the Revised Standard
Version, Catholic Edition, copyright 1946, 1952, 1957 by the
Division of Christian Education of the National Council of the
Churches of Christ in the United States of America, and are used
by permission.

Quotations of the documents of the Second Vatican Council are
from *Vatican Council II: The Conciliar and Post-Conciliar Documents*,
© 1975 by Costello Publishing Company, Inc., and Rev. Austin
Flannery, O.P., general editor.

ISBN 1–889334–24–3

First edition published in 1987 by Our Sunday Visitor, Inc.
Reprinted with permission in 2000 by
Scepter Publishers, P.O. Box 1270, Princeton, NJ 08542
Revised edition
Copyright © 2000 by Scepter Publishers

PRINTED IN THE UNITED STATES OF AMERICA

Contents

Foreword

Life is hard. Most of the world's people are miserably poor. Bad people do frightful things. Good people are imperfect and do bad things. Loved ones die. And we all know that death awaits us too. Moreover, repugnant as is the prospect of death, there are times when most of us would welcome it as an escape from pains, anxieties, and other sorts of suffering that seem unbearable.

Reality is so hard that nobody wishes to face it with both eyes wide open and unblinking. People without faith in God and without hope for Heaven try every imaginable way to evade the truth. Some, such as Marxists, accept and live according to incredible dreams that very soon humankind will enjoy Heaven on earth—without God. Others, including most Americans, try to shield themselves from suffering by wealth and status, and try to escape it with the pleasures of entertainment and recreation, food and drink, sex and drugs. But the shield is thin, and the escape, brief.

People who believe in Jesus and trust God to fulfill the Christian gospel's promises have a unique understanding of suffering and a plan for dealing with it. Indeed, this understanding and plan are the sum and substance of Christian faith and life. Yet even Christians often look at the world with an optimistic squint, focusing on reality's more agreeable aspects, as if trying to confine sin and death to some small corner of the human scene.

In my judgment, Vatican Council II did that. Influenced by the temper of its time, the great council was entirely too optimistic about the human condition, the contemporary world, and the Catholic Church itself. The extraordinary session of the synod of bishops in 1985 virtually admits as much in its final document. Having pointed out that the "signs of our time" have changed in twenty years, the synod Fathers call for a renewal of the "realism of Christian hope," and say: "It seems to us that in the present-day difficulties, God wishes to teach us more deeply the value, the importance, and the centrality of the cross of Jesus Christ."

Jesus' cross—God's paradoxical tool for overcoming human suffering—and one's personal cross, to be taken up by each and every Christian, bring sin and death to the very center of the human scene. But Jesus' cross and the crosses of those who follow him also bring into full view and proper perspective the even greater realities of forgiveness, holiness, resurrection, and everlasting life.

In this book, Russell Shaw lays out anew this Christian understanding of suffering and plan for dealing with it. He explains, develops, and applies some of the central insights of Pope John Paul II's remarkable apostolic exhortation *Salvifici doloris* (On the Christian Meaning of Human Suffering).

Shaw is not giving us another abstract, theoretical treatise on evil and suffering. Rather, he gives us a profound, compassionate, and prayerful reflection that will help people to make sense of and find value in suffering—their own and others'. The book's ultimate point is that Christians can and must accept suffering, make the most of it, and spiritually overcome it, as Jesus did. Each generation of Christians must learn how to do this, and, ultimately, each of Jesus' followers must learn the lesson for himself or herself. Thus, in offering us this work, Shaw wants it to be a starting point, not a conclusion.

Modern philosophers without faith regard the reality of evil in the world and suffering in life as their most powerful argument against the existence of a God who is not only omniscient and omnipotent but also loving. Even we believers, with our weak faith and wavering hope, are perplexed and tempted when we experience how hard reality is.

But we ought always to remember that no religion before Judaism proclaimed the existence of one Lord of all reality—a God all-knowing, all-powerful, and all-loving. That God of Abraham, Isaac, and Jacob is Jesus' God and Father, too. Thus, the unbelievers' argument against God is grounded in faith itself, and our perplexity in the face of evil and suffering is a sign of both the genuineness and the immaturity of our faith. So we must pray: "Lord, increase our faith." But we also must work to protect and nurture the faith God has given us. That is the main reason why one ought to work through a book such as this.

For serious writing dealing with a great and difficult subject, Shaw's book is easy to read. However, though popularly written, the book is unusually comprehensive. It covers, adequately for its purpose, the philosophical, scriptural, doctrinal, and practical aspects of its subject. No doubt, readers will have to work to gather and enjoy its riches. But they will find their effort rewarding.

In the face of tragedy, mature and living Christian faith is one's most valuable asset. As I write this, I think of a friend whom I visited only a few days ago. He had been having aches and pains, and the medical experts thought it was arthritis; he began to have trouble breathing, and they thought it might be tuberculosis. So he went to the hospital for tests, and they discovered cancer, which had already spread throughout his body. He is fully aware that pain and death lie ahead, yet he is serene. I am sure he will show us all how to follow the way of Jesus to the edge of this world, then leave his cross behind and leap with joyful hope into God's everlasting arms.

My earnest prayer is that every reader of this book will be helped toward such mature faith and hope, for none of us can escape suffering. But with Jesus, by the Holy Spirit's power, we can defeat suffering and win heavenly glory.

Germain Grisez
Flynn Professor of Christian Ethics
Mount Saint Mary's College
Emmitsburg, Maryland

DOES SUFFERING MAKE SENSE?

We do not belong to ourselves. Jesus Christ has bought us with his Passion and with his Death. We are his life. From now on there is only one way of living on earth: to die with Christ so as to rise again with him, to the point that we can say with the Apostle: It is not I that live, it is Christ that lives in me (Gal 2:20).

Josemaría Escrivá de Balaguer
The Way of the Cross

I

The Problem and the Mystery

Christianity takes a profoundly optimistic view of life, for it holds that something absolutely good can come from suffering. The seeds of this hope are present in the doctrine of Original Sin. It signifies, as Chesterton points out, that we have "misused a good world and not merely been entrapped into a bad one. It refers evil back to a wrong use of the will and thereby declares that it can eventually be righted by the right use of the will." In God's providence, evil and suffering—the latter being the experience of evil—can lead to something good.

Evil and suffering are, nevertheless, realities, not illusions. Ours is not the best of all possible worlds; it is merely the world God chose to create, which was, unfortunately, marred by his creatures. Something good *can* come from suffering, but often there is no tangible evidence that it does. Life remains, as Jacques Maritain says, a "wretched condition"; the difference Christianity makes is that now "the existent who vegetates in it is cut out to become God by participation."

Christianity's view of suffering is distinctively its own. Jesus Christ, who went about consoling and healing the suffering, also taught that it is good to suffer: "Blessed are the poor in spirit, for theirs is the kingdom of heaven. Blessed are those who mourn, for they shall be comforted" (Mt 5: 3–4). He himself freely accepted a miserable death as if it were necessary to accomplish the work he had set out to do. He told his followers that they must find a similar place for suffering in their lives: "If any man would come after me, let him deny himself and take up his cross and follow me." Why? Because "whoever would save his life will lose it, and whoever loses his life for my sake will find it" (Mt 16: 24–25). This formula is central to the notion of the "imitation," or "following," of Christ.

At times, in the years since the Second Vatican Council, there has been a tendency in the Church to downplay the role that suffering has in Christian life. Now that is changing. The 1985 international synod of bishops, reviewing the situation of the Church and the world in light of Vatican II, concluded that "the signs of our time" are different from those in the time of the council: "Today, in fact, everywhere in the world we witness an increase in hunger, oppression, injustice and war, sufferings, terrorism, and other forms of violence of every sort. This requires a new and more profound theological reflection."

The synod called this the "theology of the cross" —not that Christians are to exclude the theology of the creation and our Lord's Incarnation. "When we Christians speak of the cross, we do not deserve to be labeled pessimists, but we rather base ourselves upon the realism of Christian hope."

In this book I want to describe how and where suffering fits into that scheme. How can people who believe in Christianity integrate suffering into their efforts to live as Christians? What *use* can I make of suffering to become a better person, which for me as a Christian means being more like Christ?

By putting the question this way—"What use can be made of suffering?"—I do not mean to exclude from Christian life efforts to confront and vanquish suffering. Especially I have no intention of dismissing the social justice agenda of the Church, which in large measure consists of attempts to identify and eradicate the systemic causes of unjust deprivation, oppression, and the suffering they bring about. But this is not a book about injustice in society and the responsibility of the Christian to work against it. It is a book about the experience of suffering in the lives of individuals and the use they are invited to make of it.

Jesus taught that it is in some way good to suffer; but wherein does this mysterious good lie, when all our senses and our common sense, rebelling against physical or mental pain, insist that there is nothing good in this, that it has no merit at all? This book is an attempt to address the problem of suffering as it was put by the Christian apologist C. S. Lewis: "If God's goodness is inconsistent with hurting us, then either God is not good or there is no God: for in the only life we know He hurts us beyond our worst fears and beyond all we can imagine."

But that is getting ahead of the story and already beginning to speak of suffering as a Christian mystery. One can hardly begin to make sense of the "mystery" without first understanding, at least in general terms, what the "problem" of evil is.

Literature and life are full of examples to show that this problem is no mere textbook exercise but has direct, practical consequences for how people think about God and the world. Thus William James tells us: "A God who can relish such superfluities of horror is no God for human beings to appeal to." It is only a short step to Nicholas Berdyaev's contention that "the rationalist consciousness of contemporary man considers the existence of evil and suffering as the main obstacle to belief in God and the most important argument in favor of atheism."

Albert Camus, in his famous novel *The Plague*, writes a modern parable about the problem of evil. For evil he uses the metaphor of the plague, the mysterious disease that, coming from nowhere, decimates an entire city. Why do such things happen? Is there any good, any meaning, in such horrific occurrences? And if not, does it not follow that there is no goodness and no meaning in life itself, except that supplied by man through stoicism, bravery, and simple acts of kindness? A priest who is struggling to fit this episode of blind suffering into religious faith and a rationalistic doctor confront each other after leaving the bedside of a child who has died in agony. "Perhaps," the priest suggests, "we should love what we cannot understand." "No, Father," the doctor replies. "I've a very different idea of love. And until my dying day I shall refuse to love a scheme of things in which children are put to torture."

Many have said the same and go on saying it today. They are grappling with the problem of evil.

Here is how C. S. Lewis states it: "If God were good, He would wish to make His creatures perfectly happy, and if God were almighty, He would be able to do what He wished. But the creatures are not happy. Therefore God lacks either goodness, or power, or both."

There is a classic answer to this objection. In outline it is this: evil is not a positive reality but a privation; as such it does not require the causal activity of God. True, God permits this privation, evil, and the circumstances that support it, but, even so, he brings about a greater good.

In its classic form this traditional answer is not very popular today. When stated carefully, as it deserves to be, it seems too pat: an explanation capable of satisfying the mind, perhaps, but not the heart. Yet such a reaction may express failure to grasp what the explanation is saying, for it relies on a whole way of thinking about reality, a "metaphysical" *Weltanshauung*, or world view, of which people today have largely lost sight in favor of empiricism and "scientific" modes of perception and analysis.

Indeed, matters have reached the point where the traditional solution is not only rejected but caricatured. In his study of existential philosophy titled *Irrational Man*, William Barrett writes of a man who awakens one morning to find that he has suddenly, unexpectedly, gone blind: "A doctor arrives and examines his eyes. If the doctor philosophizes in the manner of Aristotle, St. Thomas, or Carnap, he will observe: the eyes are real, and the growth over the eyes is a real substance, but the non-seeing of the eyes is itself not an object and therefore not an *ens reale*, a real entity. And if doctors still know Latin or if this one has a slight touch of Molière, he may even pompously and soothingly quote St. Thomas: '*Caecitas non habet esse in rebus*' (Blindness has no being in things). For my part, I rather hope this doctor is *not* able to get out of the room fast enough to avoid the blind man's fury. His language, for all its Latin gravity, is humanly frivolous; and what is humanly frivolous ought to be somehow and somewhere philosophically wrong too."

This is effective. The difficulty is, however, that Barrett's example is itself humanly frivolous. Neither the classical account nor any other will console a person undergoing the experience of evil that is suffering. But who has ever supposed otherwise? One does not talk philosophy to a man gone suddenly blind, a woman who has lost her son, the inmates of Auschwitz, or a person with terminal cancer. The primary test of the validity of a philosophical account of evil is not whether it consoles but whether it explains.

The situation is further complicated, I suspect, by the fact that in certain moods we do not really *want* an explanation and prefer to rail against the forces of darkness and destruction, like Ahab railing against the white whale. There is a touch of showing off in announcing so grandly: "Until my dying day I shall refuse to love a scheme of things in which children are put to torture."

The classical explanation deserves better. Charles Journet, a serious and accomplished theologian, calls it "the most delicate and penetrating intellectual handling of evil the mind can attain to." By itself, it cannot relieve so much as the pain of a toothache or the frustration of missing a bus, but it can do something not necessarily less important: it can help answer the question "How can this be?"

Basic to the classical account is the insight that evil is a negation, a not-being. Not just any kind of negation, however, but a negation of a special kind: the absence of something that *should* be present. I might say, for instance, that I am subject to the negation of not-being-able-to-fly-at-will; but that particular not-being is no evil, for there is no reason to think I *ought* to be able to fly. The case is very different, however, with William Barrett's example. Blindness, the absence of sight, represents a real evil because sight, the ability to see, *ought* to be present in eyes. Evil, then, is not just not-being but privation: the absence of something that should be present.

Pope John Paul II, linking evil to the Christian view of creation and of human suffering, puts it thus: "Christianity proclaims the essential good of existence and the good of that which exists, acknowledges the goodness of the Creator, and proclaims the good of creatures. Man suffers on account of evil, which is a certain lack, limitation, or distortion of good. We could say that man suffers because of good in which he does not share, from which in a certain sense he is cut off, or of which he has deprived himself. He particularly suffers when he 'ought'—in the normal order of things—to have a share in this good and does not have it."

The insight that evil is a privation is essential to resolving the problem of how an all-good, all-powerful God can cause evil. As a matter of fact, God does *not* cause evil. For evil is a privation, an absence of being, and the absence of being does not require God's causal activity to account for it. In this explanation, Journet says: "Evil is accorded a great deal of room, so that it can be seen to its full extent, and at the same time the metaphysical poverty of evil is laid bare. But with the affirmation that evil exists, yet lacks any substance, comes the triumph over the dilemma to which those succumb who either deny the reality of evil because of God's goodness and infinite power or deny God's goodness and infinite power because of the reality of evil."

Let us consider what Journet means by "evil *exists*" and "the *reality* of evil" (emphasis mine). Although it is a privation, evil has a negative reality of its own. It is the absence of a perfection, a way of not-being that nevertheless really is present. "The paradox of evil," says Journet, "is that of 'being' and yet 'not being.' It has 'being' in the sense that it is a privation but not in the sense that it is a positive reality." That is why we experience this peculiar privation, evil, in the form of suffering: it is not merely that we lack something (I cannot fly at will) but that we lack something we ought properly to have (I cannot see). Badness is a kind of gap in something that remains good to the extent it remains the sort of thing it is—a "bad" dog or a "bad" back, for instance.

If God's causal activity is not needed to account for evil, *something* evidently is. But what? The answer, according to the classical explanation, is found in the abuse of freedom by creatures. "I think there cannot now be any doubt," St. Augustine writes, "that the only cause of any good that we enjoy is the goodness of God, and that the only cause of evil is the falling away from the unchangeable good of a being made good but changeable, first in the case of an angel, and afterward in the case of man." The source of evil, in other words, is not God's will but mine—my will and that of my fellow creatures.

According to Christian belief, the first eruption of evil into the created order came through the sin

of the angels. Obviously we do not know exactly
what happened, but we know that *something* did and
that this act of rebellion accounts for the existence
now of a malevolent angelic power, Satan, and his
followers, who involve themselves in human affairs
for the worse.

We know too that at the very dawn of human life
man also made a free choice against his best inter-
ests—that is, man sinned—and that the consequences of that choice have been transmitted to,
and multiplied among, generations since. All the
evidence indicates, as Newman said, that "the human race is implicated in some terrible aboriginal
calamity. It is out of joint with the purpose of its
existence; and thus the doctrine of what is theologi-
cally called Original Sin becomes to me almost as
certain as that the world exists and as the existence
of God." Newman, be it noted, is reflecting on facts,
evidence, of which the rest of us are all too aware; it
is false evolutionary accounts that assume the inevitability of progress—Marxism, for example—that
have the character of myth.

Our own subsequent contributions to the evil in
the world, our sins and faults of all kinds, are too
numerous and too evident to need emphasizing
here. As with the angels, as with Adam, so with us:
facing the challenge to make good use of freedom,
we often misuse it and thereby add further priva-
tions, subtractions from what ought to be, to the
negative sum of evil.

Sin, however, is not the only evil in the world.

There are innumerable natural or physical evils: ignorance, mistakes, failures, breakdowns, disease, death. It would be simplistic to think of moral evil and natural evil as absolutely separate and unrelated. It is part of the tradition, traceable to the account of the Fall in Genesis, that "natural" evils entered into human life as a result of sin; indeed that, even earlier, the angels' sin introduced disharmony and conflict into creation itself. Sin has not only personal but cosmic consequences, and the latter constitute part of the disordered "natural" environment in which we live lives marred by sufferings of many kinds.

The linkage between moral evil and cosmic, or "natural," evil is suggested by St. Paul:

> For the creation waits with eager longing for the revealing of the sons of God; for the creation was subjected to futility, not of its own will but by the will of him who subjected it in hope; because the creation itself will be set free from its bondage to decay and obtain the glorious liberty of the children of God (Rom 8: 19–21).

There is a sense, then, in which the whole created world, not only sinful mankind, stands in need of redemption from sin and the effects of sin, and it is in this sense too that all creation looks to Jesus as its only hope, since he alone is Redeemer.

The interaction between freedoms, divine, on the one hand, and angelic and human, on the other, is crucial in the case of both the sin of the angels and the sin of man. It is also profoundly mysterious— part of the reason why evil is not only a problem but, in the Christian view, a mystery properly so called.

Satan and his followers sinned freely. So did Adam. So do we. This is why the freedom of sinners distances God from responsibility for the sins and their bad consequences. But if God is the ultimate cause of everything that is, he is somehow responsible for the circumstances, however we describe them, that make evil possible.

Yet God's relationship even to the physical evil we experience is by no means that of cause to effect. The situation is described by Journet: "It is the order of the universe that God wills; punishment, which he does not will or intend—and God should not be thought of as a torturer—is the injury self-inflicted by those who rebel against an order that, being divine, could never be upset by a creature. God 'wills' it only in this quite indirect way." In other words: he permits it.

Even less is God the cause of moral evil: the opposition between God and sin is absolute. Yet God tolerates sin on the part of certain of his creatures. We can understand this apparent divine folly only by reflecting on the communion of love he desires between us and him.

Authentic adult love must establish communion by mutual self-giving. There is and can be no such love without freedom. No one can be coerced into loving another. No one can make the gift of self without being aware of the possibility of its being refused, yet freely choosing to give it. Either love exists freely or it does not exist at all.

But a world in which there could be no sin would be one that excluded the freedom to give or to refuse the gift of self. Philosophers and theologians argue about whether God could have created such a world, but the fact is that he did not. We may suppose he did not because, among other reasons, to have done so would have excluded love as well as freedom. Is our freedom (and therefore the possibility, now the actuality, of sin and its consequences) too high a price to pay to make love possible? Whatever our opinion, God's answer evidently is No.

Before leaving the philosophical and theological accounts of evil behind us, we need to consider another way of viewing the question, one that is popular today. As we have seen, the traditional way of accounting for evil has its problems, including the problem that it can seem too pat, especially when (as is certainly true of the brief sketch just given) it skims lightly over profound depths and attempts to shed a "reasonable" and "positive" light on darkly shadowed areas. Partly in reaction to this treatment and partly in response to modern intellectual currents, particularly the impact of evolutionary thinking, "process theology" has emerged to give an alternate account of evil and suffering.

In 1982 a book titled *When Bad Things Happen to Good People* appeared and quickly achieved enormous popularity. People are still reading it. The work of Rabbi Harold S. Kushner, it tells how he and his family came to terms with the fact that his much loved son, Aaron, was suffering from progeria, a rare condition that causes rapid aging in children. Rabbi Kushner was told that Aaron "would never grow much beyond three feet in height, would have no hair on his head or body, would look like a little old man while he was still a child, and would die in his early teens." The father's first response was one most of us would make: "If God existed, if he was minimally fair, let alone loving and forgiving, how could he do this to me?"

The book is an answer to that question, in many respects a wise and helpful answer. In line with biblical teaching, especially that of the Book of Job, Rabbi Kushner rejects the notion that our sufferings are punishments inflicted on us by God. Similarly, he sets aside explanations that try to find the "good" in suffering ("it will make you more thoughtful . . . more sensitive . . . a better person") partly to console those who suffer but also, and perhaps mainly, to make excuses for God. "It may be true," he writes, "that sometimes we have to do painful things to people we love for their benefit, but not every painful thing that happens to us is beneficial."

Most important, perhaps, he makes a point that the classical account also is at pains to make: God is not the cause of evil and ordinarily cannot be said to send us our sufferings. Here, though, the classical account and the process-theology approach of Rabbi Kushner part company. The former, recognizing God as all-wise and all-powerful, deals with the fact of evil by arguing that God permits or tolerates it in order to respect the freedom he bestows on certain of his creatures; at the same time, he contrives to bring good—indeed, greater good —even out of evil. Process theology tries to cope with the same problem by arguing that, in one way or another, God is less wise or less powerful than Jews and Christians generally believe: "God would like people to get what they deserve in life, but he cannot always arrange it."

How do we explain this argument? Perhaps creation itself—that is, "the process of replacing chaos with order"—has not been completed. God still has work to do, or he may have done all the work he intends to do and now may be leaving it to us to finish the job. (In fact, there is an important element of truth in this theory.) Meanwhile, the world as it stands is incomplete, a less-than-perfect place where bad things happen not because of divine malevolence but because of the incompleteness of creation. Bad things "happen at random, and randomness is another name for chaos, in those corners of the universe where God's creative light has not yet penetrated. And chaos is evil; not wrong, not malevolent, but evil nonetheless, because by causing tragedies at random, it prevents people from believing in God's goodness."

Although *When Bad Things Happen to Good People* scarcely breaks fresh theological ground, it is a popular and attractive presentation of a point of view, influential in theological circles, that has much to recommend it. To the extent that it represents a reaction against a way of talking about God that robs him of mystery and lets us imagine we really know what it means for him to be "all-powerful," it has the character of a needed corrective. But this point of view also involves serious theological problems of its own, especially when it asserts in at least one of its versions that God is not all-powerful. "He does the best He can," says Kushner, "but the world in a profound sense is out of control."

More promising, as I have suggested, is an approach that, instead of changing our view of God, suggests a more nuanced view of the world: the world as it now exists cannot be without some failures; evil and suffering are statistically inevitable here; and it is unreasonable, certainly contradictory, to suggest that even an all-powerful God can do the impossible and eliminate evil and suffering from such a world.

Just how altered a view of the world does this amount to? The Christian tradition has always considered the world a radically flawed place, where life inevitably involves much misery, even for the "happiest" of men and women. The tradition has never regarded this as the best of all possible worlds, but only the world as it is, marred by creatures' sins, a world God now invites us to join him in renewing and bringing, with much difficulty and pain, to the final consummation he intends. The tradition does not share the deists' view that God as Creator brought the world—that is, the universe—into being as a kind of enormous mechanical system, complete and self-contained, which he leaves to its own devices. Rather, the work of creation continues, and we are co-creators with God, participants in his creative work, so that the outcome of creation may now be said to rest somehow and to some extent in our imperfect hands.

In other words, creation as it stands is not complete, not in its final and definitive form, not as it ultimately shall be, and suffering is one unavoidable offshoot of the process by which both the world and we, as creatures in the world, although seriously crippled by sin, now change and grow toward final fulfillment. "We know that the whole creation has been groaning in travail together until now; and not only the creation, but we ourselves, who have the first fruits of the Spirit, groan inwardly as we wait for adoption as sons, the redemption of our bodies" (Rom 8:22–23).

Here, however, one must be extremely cautious and avoid a simpleminded apologetic that would seem to brush aside sin and suffering as matters of little importance or, even worse, suggest that they are somehow good and desirable in themselves. Faith does not offer superficial consolation. Even though "in everything God works for good with those who love him" (Rom 8:28), still it is difficult and often even impossible, humanly speaking, to see *how* good can come from the miseries that have afflicted the human race throughout history and that darken our own lives.

What "good" did the Holocaust promote, wherein some six million Jews were murdered by the Nazis? Where is the increment to human happiness in the death of a child, in the agony of physical or mental illness, in the latest natural disaster, in the most recent instance of man's inhumanity to man? We simply do not know. God, being all-wise and all-powerful, can bring good out of all these evils, but in most cases we do not know how he does it. We are thrown back on Job's answer: God *is* good, and he altogether surpasses our understanding. But it is important not to waver in affirming what we do know: God does bring good out of evil, even though usually we cannot see this happening.

It is also important to keep clearly in mind the distinction between evil and suffering, which is the experience of evil. Suffering is essentially a disagreeable and undesired state of consciousness, something we undergo without wanting it. But it is not doing evil, nor does it even include the evil that is experienced (the pain of my toothache is one thing, the disease of the tooth, which has reached the point of attacking a nerve, is something quite different).

Being the kind of creatures we are, we tend to regard suffering, not evil, as the worst thing there is and to be more anxious to avoid the former than the latter. Hence, the plausibility of utilitarianism and its ethical offshoots, which equate good with the removal or avoidance of suffering and legitimize doing evil in pursuit of this supposedly supreme objective. The consequences, for ethical thinking and much else, have been disastrous.

Suffering is useful and necessary for keeping us in touch with the objective facts of our human condition. Physical sufferings like toothaches and burns illustrate the point. The pain is a signal that something is wrong and an urgent reminder to take corrective action. People with nervous disorders that make it difficult or impossible to experience pain are frighteningly vulnerable to physical injuries they may not even notice until it is too late.

We can see something similar at work in the case of the mental suffering involved in objectively based repugnance, fear, guilt, and remorse. Particularly where such feelings pertain to one's own real sinfulness, they most often provide the initial incentive either to avoid sin or, if one has fallen, to repent and ask God's pardon. In the Old Testament, Pope John Paul says, we begin to find an understanding of suffering that goes beyond seeing it simply as punishment for sin and perceives its "educational" value. "Thus in the sufferings inflicted by God upon the Chosen People there is included an invitation of his mercy, which corrects in order to lead to conversion: 'These punishments were designed not to destroy but to discipline our people' (2 Mac 6: 12)."

33

There is, however, a much more profound fact about suffering. Even where it is impossible to discern an educational value in the experience, God brings good out of the evil and suffering that he permits. Says St. Augustine: "The Almighty God, who, as even the heathen acknowledge, has supreme power over all things, being himself supremely good, would never permit the existence of anything evil among his works, if he were not so omnipotent and good that he can bring good even out of evil."

In fact, not only does God bring good out of evil, he brings about a greater good than if the evil had never occurred. One might say that God is constantly remodeling creation in order to draw it through the chaos and pain of evil to a state of perfection higher than if his original plan had been left intact, uncontradicted by the evil choices of creatures and the consequences flowing from them.

This is true even, and perhaps especially, in regard to sin. According to St. Thomas Aquinas:

> Nothing prevents human nature being raised to a higher state after sin. God permits, indeed, that evils come about so as to draw a greater good from them. Whence the words of St. Paul to the Romans, 5:20: "Where sin increased, grace abounded all the more." And the cry of the Exsultet: *O felix culpa, O happy fault, that deserved so great a Redeemer!*

At this point we have traveled far beyond both everyday experience and philosophical arguments in attempting to understand evil and suffering; we have entered the realm of faith. It is here, however, that the metaphysical accounts of evil must lead. Metaphysics examines evil as a "problem"; faith, which does not dismiss metaphysics but raises the discussion to a different plane, probes evil and suffering as elements of Christian mystery.

In ordinary speech a "mystery" is a kind of puzzle to be solved. Agatha Christie wrote mysteries in this sense. Christians, however, do not view the mysteries of faith as the religious equivalents of a detective story. Rather, a mystery of faith pertains to the story of salvation; it is an aspect of God's wise and loving plan of creation and redemption. Christ and his kingdom are the heart of that plan, hidden until revealed by God in Jesus' life, death, and Resurrection. The truth of a mystery is too far beyond our limited human experience for us to comprehend it fully. This does not mean we can understand nothing about mysteries, but it certainly means we cannot understand everything.

The mystery of suffering stands out with unique, unrepeatable starkness in the life of Jesus himself, the Jesus of Gethsemane, of the *praetorium*, of Golgotha. Why should *this* have happened to *him*?

If we do once ask this question, the suffering of Jesus seems at first glance to make little or no sense—indeed, to constitute a virtually insuperable obstacle to faith. Yet Christians from the beginning unhesitatingly have insisted that precisely the experience of suffering and death is central to the meaning of Christ's life as well as to the religion he founded.

> For Jews demand signs and Greeks seek wisdom, but we preach Christ crucified, a stumbling block to Jews and folly to Gentiles, but to those who are called, both Jews and Greeks, Christ the power of God and the wisdom of God. For the foolishness of God is wiser than men, and the weakness of God is stronger than men (1 Cor 1:22–25).

The problem, however, goes even beyond finding the meaning and the positive fruit (if any) that suffering has in the life of Christ; it extends to finding the same in the suffering of Christians. Christian life can be described as the "following," or "imitation," of Christ, and it seems clear that our suffering is, in some way, of central importance to our efforts to imitate him.

We have Jesus' own word for this.

> If any man would come after me, let him deny himself and take up his cross and follow me. For whoever would save his life will lose it; and whoever loses his life for my sake and the gospel's will save it (Mk 8:34–35).

> He who does not take his cross and follow me is not worthy of me (Mt 10:38).

> Truly, truly, I say to you, unless a grain of wheat falls into the earth and dies, it remains alone; but if it dies, it bears much fruit. He who loves his life loses it, and he who hates his life in this

world will keep it for eternal life. If any one
serves me, he must follow me; and where I am,
there shall my servant be also (Jn 12:24–26).

Such passages dot the Gospels like stations in the
Way of the Cross. Jesus time and again seeks to
impress on his first disciples and (through them)
on us the same startling message: he must suffer, we
who propose to follow him must also suffer, and his
suffering and ours are linked; moreover, the experience of suffering and defeat marks out, both for
him and for us, the route to victory and fulfillment.
There is no other way. Jesus must die before he can
rise; so must we.

Also repeated and elaborated throughout the
New Testament is the theme of intimate, extraordinary linkage between Christ and Christians, especially in this experience of suffering: "I have been
crucified with Christ; it is no longer I who live, but
Christ who lives in me" (Gal 2:20). Suffering is
necessary, indeed central, in Christian life: "For to
this you have been called, because Christ also suffered for you, leaving you an example, that you
should follow in his steps" (1 Pet 2:21). Fulfillment
is ultimately achieved through suffering: "As we
have shared much in the suffering of Christ, so
through Christ do we share abundantly in his consolation" (2 Cor 1:5). The New Testament is a book
of good news, not a book of suffering; but part of its
good news is that suffering has been endowed by
Jesus Christ with immense positive meaning and
value.

In fact, as Pope John Paul observes, suffering has not only one but two Christian meanings. The first concerns the suffering we ourselves experience, while the second concerns the suffering of other people and our response to it. These two Christian meanings of suffering are the focus of the Holy Father's 1984 apostolic exhortation *Salvifici doloris* (On the Christian Meaning of Human Suffering), which led me to write this book.

Our suffering is a way for us to participate in the redemptive work of Christ. At the root of this reality is our membership in Christ's Mystical Body. We are not isolated individuals, focused on ourselves in selfish gratification or meaningless self-torment. We are "members" of Christ and also of one another; we can participate in his acts and help others share in their merits.

We do this preeminently in the Mass, where, if we really take part actively in mind and heart, we participate—we become partners—in Jesus' own perfect act of self-giving to the Father. But this is true not only at Mass; it is true also of the other worthy actions and experiences of our lives.

It is true even, or perhaps especially, of our suffering borne for love. St. Paul writes, "Now I rejoice in my sufferings for your sake, and in my flesh I complete what is lacking in Christ's afflictions for the sake of his body, that is, the church" (Col 1:24). Not that there was something defective in Jesus' suffering; it was perfectly efficacious, fully able to accomplish its redemptive purpose. But Jesus' human suffering did not exhaust all human suffering; his individual body is not his whole Mystical Body. *We* suffer too. When we accept suffering—when we bear it patiently, courageously, and lovingly—we suffer with Christ; in doing so, we complete his suffering in his complete Body, which is the Church, and we receive in our lives and extend into the lives of others the redeeming value of his suffering.

In view of all this, it is no coincidence that the cross is the symbol of Christianity. The cross is not merely a kind of patriotic symbol, like the flag, or even a historical reminder of how Jesus lived and died. It is a sign of how we, as followers of Christ, are also meant to live—and die.

There is nothing morbid about this thought, nor is it an expression of passive and unhealthy resignation in the face of suffering and evil. Critics of Christianity sometimes accuse its adherents of just this fault: confronted with human misery, Christians are likely to sigh, lower their eyes, and murmur, "God's will be done." This caricature has a kernel of truth. In practice, there is a fine line between accepting and finding value in unavoidable suffering and taking a passive, or complacent, attitude toward suffering, especially toward the suffering of someone else. In general, a good motto for Christian life is, "Avoid the suffering that can be avoided rightly and remedy the suffering that can be remedied rightly. But learn to accept and make

39

use of the suffering that, without doing evil, can neither be avoided nor remedied."

All this applies in a special way when it comes to the second Christian meaning of suffering: our response to the suffering of others. Here, above all, we may not be passive and indifferent. Nor may we indulge in the insensitive and, in many cases, literally scandalous smugness of doing nothing except preach "resignation." Instead, we must do what we can to help.

We have a model in the parable of the Good Samaritan. "It indicates," Pope John Paul says,

> what the relationship of each of us must be toward our suffering neighbor. We are not allowed to "pass by on the other side" indifferently; we must "stop" beside him. Everyone who stops beside the suffering of another person, whatever form it may take, is a Good Samaritan. This stopping does not mean curiosity but availability.

Pope John Paul's *Salvifici doloris* attaches particular importance to the passage quoted above from St. Paul's letter to the Colossians (1:24)—"I complete what is lacking in Christ's afflictions for the sake of his body, that is, the church." The Holy Father writes:

> These words seem to be found at the end of the long road that winds through the suffering which forms part of the history of man and which is illuminated by the Word of God. These

words have, as it were, the value of a final discovery, which is accompanied by joy. . . . The joy comes from the discovery of the meaning of suffering, and this discovery, even if it is most personally shared in by Paul of Tarsus, who wrote these words, is at the same time valid for others. The Apostle shares his own discovery and rejoices in it because of all those whom it can help—just as it helped him—to understand *the salvific meaning of suffering.*

By suffering we can become co-redeemers with Christ, participate in his redemptive act, expiate our own sins, and contribute to the process by which the merits of the redemption are extended to others. Even at the risk of being misunderstood, one must say that suffering occupies a privileged place in Christian life.

But the risk of misunderstanding evidently *is* very real. It is impossible to read some of the "spiritual" literature on this subject without finding notions that seem strange by any standards. We must avoid falling into the same traps.

One is the trap of being too "reasonable" and "clear" about suffering. I wish to explain how we become co-redeemers with Christ through the experience of suffering; I hope to give as lucid an account as I can. But there is a danger of treating co-redemption and membership in Christ in almost mechanical terms, as if they were remarkable clocks whose cases we remove in order to examine the network of springs, wheels, and levers within.

One can, in fact, find theological and ascetical

writing that proceeds in this manner, reducing the subtle interplay of grace, free will, and intellect to a process not unlike the functioning of clockwork. Yet, as we shall see, the realities under consideration here more nearly resemble the exquisitely sensitive and varied functioning of an organism than the lifeless regularity of even the most sophisticated machine.

There is also the risk of seeming to become a kind of advocate for suffering, as if the experience of evil were a good and desirable thing in its own right. This too is something one finds in a certain kind of religious literature, whose pious authors probably did not mean to give this impression but, in their enthusiasm to point out the advantages that can come from suffering, fell into the trap of singing its praises.

There is nothing wrong with this enthusiasm, provided we understand that it is not precisely suffering that is to be praised but the good that can be realized through suffering and as a result of it. Unfortunately, though, not everyone who writes on this subject makes that clear; and where it is not clear, Christianity can be made to sound as if it rejoices in pain for pain's sake.

Charity, not suffering, is central to Christianity and to the interior life of the Christian. It would be not merely false but dangerous to attempt to base a spirituality on suffering—as great a perversion as is the contemporary effort to found a spirituality on psychological "fulfillment" and "feeling good about oneself." The genius of Christian spirituality is its balance and, especially, its transcendence. Both pain and "feeling good" have places in it, but, ultimately, it is not one's subjective state—one's feelings—that is important but the deeper aspects of one's personal relationship with God.

That said, however, the role of suffering in the interior life needs constant emphasis: not suffering alone, of course, but suffering linked to charity, suffering accepted, even welcomed, out of love. The model is Christ. "Look at our Lord," urges Dom Columba Marmion. "He made no act of love more intense than when in his glory he accepted the bitter chalice offered to him, and when, abandoned by his Father, he achieved his sacrifice upon the Cross."

This way of speaking is out of fashion today, when most sermons and popular religious writing emphasize only the "good news" aspects of Christianity. So much the worse for today's sermons and popular religious writing! Programmed optimism not only trivializes Christianity, by trivializing sin and its consequences (and, therefore, trivializing the redemption from sin won by Christ: for if the disease is a small thing, so must be the cure), it also fails, as everyone knows quite well, to do three indispensable things: first, to come to grips with the wrenching facts of defeat, sickness, pain, tragedy, and death; second, to find a place for these realities in our efforts to lead Christian lives; and third, to provide us with any real consolation in our suffering or any particular incentive to put suffering to good use as a means for growth in holiness.

The main consequence of such preaching and popular religious writing is to reinforce the secular humanist view that sees suffering as the supreme evil to be avoided at all costs. Yet suffering, as we have seen, is not evil but the *experience* of evil. The supreme evil is sin. As for suffering, while it is not something to be sought after, it can have beneficial results, recognizable even by a secularist: for example, it can remind us to do something about the evil that is causing us to suffer.

Often enough, too, avoiding suffering "at all costs" means at all costs to other people. We stand ready, it seems, to do almost anything for the sake of escaping some trouble, some pain, for ourselves. Hence, the popularity today of murderous solutions (from legalized abortion to nuclear deterrence) to a host of individual and social problems.

In the argument between faith and nonfaith, believers not infrequently make things more difficult for themselves than they have to be. Their opponents use suffering as an argument against God precisely by importing concepts from *faith* (God is all-good, all-knowing, all-powerful) and challenging believers to show how these attributes can be squared with the fact of evil; but believers try to respond by using purely rational arguments instead of considerations drawn from the same source the nonbelievers have mined: faith. There are, indeed, valid, rational arguments in this debate, yet suffering ultimately is a challenge to move from a faith that is weak to a faith that is strong.

To understand ourselves and make sense of our lives, we must look to Christ, who, in the words of the Second Vatican Council, "fully reveals man to himself and makes his supreme calling clear." What is true in general is also true of suffering in particular: to make sense of suffering, we must look to Christ and find the meaning that suffering had for him. "At one and the same time," Pope John Paul says, "Christ has taught man to do good by his suffering and to do good to those who suffer. In this double aspect he has completely revealed the meaning of suffering."

What use shall we make of suffering in order to become more like Christ? That is a practical, sensible question. "If suffer we must," Caryll Houselander once remarked, "it seems at least as reasonable to do it well as it is to speak well or to walk or sleep well." But there is another, higher reason for trying to suffer well: co-redemption—the expiation of sin, one's own and that of others. "My personal suffering," Houselander added, "can lighten the world's sorrow, by redeeming the world's sin. If you are baptized you are a Christ, to be 'christened' does literally mean that, to be Christ-ened. Because we are each of us a Christ, our sorrows are his Passion continuing in the world."

It is humbling to read this sort of thing. One

believes, but one doesn't measure up. Finally, it is as C. S. Lewis said: "When pain is to be borne, a little courage helps more than much knowledge, a little human sympathy more than much courage, and the least tincture of the love of God more than all."

II

Suffering in the Life of Christ

To understand suffering in the life of the Christian, one must understand its place in the life and teaching of Jesus Christ, for, as Pope John Paul II says, "Christ causes us to enter into the mystery and to discover the 'why' of suffering." But to appreciate the radical newness of Jesus' view of suffering, it is necessary to set it in the perspective of what came before: the perspective, that is, of the Old Testament.

One view reflected in the Old Testament is that suffering is punishment that God metes out to us for our sins. Perhaps it has corrective value, perhaps not. In any case, both individually and collectively we bring our miseries on ourselves by offending God and provoking him to punish us. But this view is balanced by an awareness that matters often do not work out so neatly: the wicked enjoy success, while the good suffer and decline. The ambivalence this produces is captured in Psalm 73:

> But, as for me, my feet had almost stumbled, my steps had well nigh slipped. For I was envious of the arrogant, when I saw the prosperity of the

wicked. . . . All in vain I have kept my heart clean and washed my hands in innocence. For all the day long I have been stricken, and chastened every morning (Ps 73: 2–3, 13–14).

It is hardly surprising that the Old Testament writers did not arrive quickly and easily at the solution to a problem that, in fact, only God's revelation in Jesus Christ provides. We should congratulate them on their tenacity and subtlety in wrestling with the problem, and we should appropriate for ourselves the truth of their responses to it. That is certainly the case with the Book of Job.

Job is a theological dialogue, a kind of drama, whose protagonist confronts the inadequacy of the explanation that suffering is punishment for personal sin. This explanation makes no sense in the case of good people who suffer. Instead, various alternatives are proposed, or hinted at, in setting out the story of a virtuous man whom God allows to be tried by dreadful afflictions. It is possible to read Job in several ways, but the most straightforward and satisfying reading is that, when all is said and done, we overreach ourselves in trying to "explain" suffering. God knows; we don't.

Near the end of the dialogue God says to Job:

Where were you when I laid the foundation of the earth? Tell me, if you have understanding. Who determined its measurements—surely you know! Or who stretched the line upon it? On what were its bases sunk, or who laid the cornerstone, when the morning stars sang together

and all the sons of God shouted for joy? . . . Shall
a faultfinder contend with the Almighty? He
who argues with God, let him answer it (Job
38: 4–7; 40: 2).

And Job replies:

I know that thou canst do all things, and that no
purpose of thine can be thwarted. . . . Therefore
I have uttered what I did not understand, things
too wonderful for me, which I did not know. . . .
I had heard of thee by the hearing of the ear, but
now my eye sees thee; therefore I despise myself,
and repent in dust and ashes (Job 42: 2–6).

There is much wisdom in that answer. We know very
little about God by our own reason and experience
and a good deal more because God has chosen to
tell us about himself, but there is much else that
remains mysterious about God, altogether beyond
our reason and experience in this life. In certain
aspects, God's reasons for permitting evil and suffering fall into that category. We should not pre-
tend to have answers for things that, for us, are
unanswerable. Why do the Jobs of the world suffer?
"God only knows" is a good reply.

Even in the Old Testament, however, a better
reply begins to emerge. Isaiah sketches a mysterious
figure, the Suffering Servant, whose misery and
death are in some way expiatory and redemptive. In
due course, Jesus will explicitly apply to himself
what Isaiah says of the Suffering Servant—"He was
counted among the wicked" (Lk 22: 37)—and
Christians have traditionally read these passages in

the Good Friday liturgy as moving and singularly apt prophecies concerning Christ:

> He had no form or comeliness that we should
>   look at him,
>   and no beauty that we should desire him.
> He was despised and rejected by men,
>   a man of sorrows, and acquainted with grief;
> and as one from whom men hide their faces
>   he was despised, and we esteemed him not.
>
> Surely he has borne our griefs
>   and carried our sorrows;
> yet we esteemed him stricken,
>   smitten by God, and afflicted.
> But he was wounded for our transgressions,
>   he was bruised for our iniquities;
> upon him was the chastisement that made us
>   whole,
>   and with his stripes we are healed.
> All we like sheep have gone astray;
>   we have turned every one to his own way;
> and the LORD has laid on him
>   the iniquity of us all. . . .
>
> By his knowledge shall the righteous one, my
>   servant,
>   make many to be accounted righteous;
>   and he shall bear their iniquities.
>
> Is 53: 2–6, 11

No longer is suffering a punishment for the sin of the one who suffers. No longer is the suffering of the innocent an incomprehensible divine quirk that human beings not only cannot understand but have no right to question. In the figure of the

Suffering Servant, suffering becomes rich with meaning, a paradoxical source of the most profound consolation. "It can be said," Pope John Paul writes, "that this is 'substitutive' suffering; but above all it is 'redemptive.' The Man of Sorrows of that prophecy is truly that 'Lamb of God who takes away the sin of the world.'"

What, then, is the meaning of suffering in the life of Jesus Christ? What does he teach on the matter? How does he respond to suffering when he encounters it in others? Above all, what role does suffering play in his own experience and in the accomplishment of his mission?

While Christians turn naturally to the Gospels for answers, this seems an odd and irrelevant exercise to many persons today. They have no particular hostility toward Jesus; indeed, if pressed, they might say sincerely that he was a remarkable man in many ways: an individual of exalted idealism, profound wisdom, and unusual benevolence; a man too good for this tarnished world who, like many such others, suffered persecution and death on that account.

But would these same people turn to Jesus and the records of Christian faith for the explanation of human experience and the key to dealing with it? Not likely. Instead, the argument offered by such people often sounds something like this: "I don't look to Jesus or anybody else for that kind of help. I'll either find the meaning of my life myself or I won't find any meaning in it at all. And, to tell the truth, I think the latter is more likely than the former."

The twentieth century saw a great change in the way people write and read biographies. Biographers used to present the lives of exemplary persons for our instruction and imitation. Now their purpose is apparently to demonstrate that the great (or, at least, the notorious) are as flawed as we who read about them. The new approach has literary and historical advantages; it is certainly an improvement over merely adulatory biographies (including some of the saints) that bend or suppress facts so as to depict their subjects as faultless. But it has its own problems.

At its roots, I think, lies something approaching self-hatred. The implication is that even the most distinguished among us are rather awful. Viciousness, infidelity, intemperance, madness: these are all but universal traits among even our best and brightest. God help the rest of us!

Whence comes this collective self-hatred? Darwin and Freud? Perhaps. Distinguished scientists though they were, their theories have, among other things, undermined our confidence in ourselves as superior beings whose faults and flaws are no more than anomalies in a basic pattern of upward aspiration and achievement. And, if there were any serious doubts about the matter, the record of the twentieth century—two world wars, the threat of an unimaginably worse war, genocidal massacres in totalitarian states, massive legalized abortion in the "liberal" West, Hitler, Stalin, the Khmer Rouge, perversion and lunacy rampant—seems to settle it: we are vicious, murderous animals who threaten one another and ourselves.

In some ways it *is* difficult to turn from this evaluation to the life of Jesus. Murderous viciousness abounds in the Gospels too, but at the center of the story, transcending all, stands the figure of Christ, this extraordinary, suffering man whom we know we cannot emulate, but whom we would give our lives to resemble. Peter—unselfconscious Peter, whose spontaneity may in the end have been his salvation—speaks for the rest of us. "Jesus said to the twelve, 'Will you also go away?' Simon Peter answered him, 'Lord, to whom shall we go? You have the words of eternal life; and we have believed, and have come to know, that you are the Holy One of God' " (Jn 6:67–69). Even in his suffering. Especially in his suffering.

Let us begin by considering what Jesus taught about suffering.

He taught, first, that it was necessary for him to suffer. "From that time Jesus began to show his disciples that he must go to Jerusalem and suffer many things from the elders and chief priests and scribes, and be killed, and on the third day be raised" (Mt 16:21). This message, needless to say, was not well received by those closest to him. They were looking for an all-conquering messiah-king who would restore Israel to greatness and, not least, carry them along to the heights. Talk of suffering and death was not what they wanted to hear.

Jesus, for his own part, although he was God, was also man, as human as you and I. He saw perfectly the attractiveness of not pursuing a line of action that would lead ultimately to his Passion and death. Jesus, like us, was subject to temptation, even though, unlike us, he did not succumb. Is there a greater temptation than the suggestion to evade suffering that one ought to accept?

Jesus also taught that it was necessary for his followers to suffer—not only his first disciples but all who would come after, all who, until the end of time, would try to model their lives and their selves on him. "If any man would come after me, let him deny himself and take up his cross and follow me. For whoever would save his life will lose it, and whoever loses his life for my sake will find it" (Mt 16: 24–25).

We may suppose that such teaching was not received with warm enthusiasm by his disciples, any more than were his predictions of his own suffering and death. It is the same today. Now, as then, even the promises linked by Jesus to this doctrine—above all, the promise of resurrection and eternal life—are scarcely able to neutralize the immediate prospect of suffering.

The disciples simply could not take it in. Jesus' words about his suffering, death, and Resurrection were incomprehensible to them at first. Nor were they able immediately to grasp the idea that suffering and death would be associated with their following of Jesus. It is the same with us. For, while it is fairly easy to give intellectual assent to the proposition that suffering has a place in the Christian scheme of things, when it comes to its place in *my* life . . . thank you, but I'd rather not.

Finally, and perhaps most difficult to comprehend and accept, Jesus taught that suffering is in some sense a good thing: at least to the extent that it is the necessary prelude to final fulfillment. The message is clear in the Sermon on the Mount, that remarkable compendium of Jesus' teaching with which Matthew launches his account of the proclamation of the reign of God, announced by Jesus and embodied in him (Mt 5:3–12):

> Blessed are the poor in spirit, for theirs is the
>   kingdom of heaven.
> Blessed are those who mourn, for they shall be
>   comforted.
> Blessed are the meek, for they shall inherit the
>   earth.
> Blessed are those who hunger and thirst for
>   righteousness, for they shall be satisfied.
> Blessed are the merciful, for they shall obtain
>   mercy.
> Blessed are the pure in heart, for they shall see
>   God.
> Blessed are the peacemakers, for they shall be
>   called sons of God.
> Blessed are those who are persecuted for
>   righteousness' sake, for theirs is the
>   kingdom of heaven.
> Blessed are you when men revile you and
>   persecute you and utter all kinds of evil

against you falsely on my account. Rejoice
and be glad, for your reward is great in
heaven, for so men persecuted the prophets
who were before you.

We are a long way here from the ethic of success,
which is so widely and uncritically accepted today.
These words of Jesus introduce us to a different
value system, one that holds up worldly wisdom to
inspection and finds it wanting. The teaching of the
beatitudes is that suffering and happiness are not
incompatible; suffering can *contribute* to happiness.
It is true that the happiness of those who suffer is,
manifestly, not complete: fulfillment comes only in
Heaven. But the happiness of those who suffer for
love of God begins here below.

Even though this message lies at the heart of
Jesus' teaching about suffering, it should not be
supposed that Jesus sought out his own suffering
for its own sake. It is a wretched thing to suffer;
one who perceives value in the experience rebels
at the same time against the misery of it. Jesus certainly did.

> And he came out, and went, as was his custom,
> to the Mount of Olives; and the disciples fol-
> lowed him. And when he came to the place he
> said to them, "Pray that you may not enter into
> temptation." And he withdrew from them about
> a stone's throw, and knelt down and prayed,
> "Father, if thou art willing, remove this cup from
> me; nevertheless not my will but thine be done."
> . . . And being in an agony he prayed more ear-
> nestly, and his sweat became like great drops of

blood falling down upon the ground (Lk 22:39–
42, 44).

Jesus' prayer consists of two parts: that he be spared
this suffering and that God's will be done. We can
be sure he meant both parts.

There is also much to be learned from Jesus' attitude toward the suffering of others. It is compassionate, but it is hardly sentimental. Coming upon a
widow who has lost her only son, he "has compassion on her" and tells her, "Do not weep," before
restoring the young man to life (Luke 7:11–15).
Confronted with a Canaanite woman whose daugh-
ter is "severely possessed by a demon," he at first
ignores her, then brusquely dismisses her ("It is not
fair to take the children's bread and throw it to the
dogs") because his mission is to Israel. Only when
she shows her "great faith" does he grant the relief
she seeks (Mt 15:22–28). Jesus cured many and
alleviated much suffering; but he did not go out of
his way to cure all those he could have cured or to
remove all pain and grief, either for his contemporaries or for us. Jesus, it seems, is more immediately
interested in pointing out the place of suffering in
life than in eliminating it.

This is true even with his miracles of healing.
They are individual acts of compassion directed to
particular persons, unique manifestations of Jesus'
love for each one. But they also have a didactic
purpose: first, to show the nearness of God's kingdom and to teach who Jesus is; and, second, to

teach the place that evil and suffering will hence-
forth occupy in the coming of the kingdom, which
Jesus inaugurates with his Passion, death, Resurrection, and Ascension.

Evil and suffering remain oppressive realities in
life, yet their previously firm grip on human destiny
has been broken; they are in disarray, retreat; their
days are numbered. This is the message of the
miracles. "Suffering is not eternal," Charles Journet
writes, "but is destined in the divine plan to be
overcome and eliminated. And so, to mark the
precariousness of its reign and the fact that physical
evil has not always been man's lot but rather was
forced upon him, Christ on certain occasions cast it
out with a single word." These acts of healing are
signs that, in God's plan, beyond suffering lie resto-
ration and fulfillment.

"Yet," adds Journet, "Christ's immediate purpose
was not to remove suffering but to take it upon
himself and light it up from within." More important than how he did away with the suffering of
others in certain cases is how he underwent suffering himself. We learn the role that suffering is
meant to play in our lives by pondering the role it
played in the life of Jesus Christ, a role he inter-
preted for us by his explicit teaching.

Let us start with an obvious fact: Jesus' life was a
hard one. There was, for one thing, the universal
hardness of the time and place. True, notions of
physical comfort and discomfort vary from indi-

vidual to individual and society to society, and Jesus and his contemporaries saw nothing remarkable or disagreeable about circumstances that we, accustomed to pampering, would find unbearable; but it is also true that, for all but a very few persons of great wealth, life in that particular time and place was precarious and often painful. The vast majority of the people, Henri Daniel-Rops observes, were "poor, and even very poor . . . in reading the Gospels one has the impression of great economic stringency." Such conveniences as central heating and indoor plumbing were unheard of. The typical rural house—the sort of dwelling we may suppose Jesus, Mary, and Joseph shared in Nazareth—was "a rudimentary affair, a whitewashed cube with few openings, perhaps none except the door, and a single room inside, divided into two, one half for the animals, the other for the family."

Life expectancy was short, disease rampant, medicine primitive. Although the Gospel accounts make it clear that diabolical possession was a fact, we can suppose that many cases of severe mental illness were mistaken for possession and handled with what we now recognize as harshness.

Even against this background, though, Jesus' life manifests aspects of suffering that are peculiarly his. What must it have meant for him, a man of genius and profound religious and moral sensitivity, to grow up and live most of his life in a remote backwoods village like Nazareth, surrounded for the most part, one can only suppose, by neighbors and companions who, to put it charitably, were wanting in social graces and intellectual refinement? One gets some hint of the setting for these years of Jesus' life from the Gospel account of his return to Nazareth after his public life has begun and his fame has spread.

> He . . . came to his own country; and his disciples followed him. And on the sabbath he began to teach in the synagogue; and many who heard him were astonished, saying, "Where did this man get all this? What is the wisdom given to him? What mighty works are wrought by his hands! Is not this the carpenter, the son of Mary and brother of James and Joses and Judas and Simon, and are not his sisters here with us?" And they took offense at him. And Jesus said to them, "A prophet is not without honor, except in his own country, and among his own kin, and in his own house." And he could do no mighty work there, except that he laid his hands upon a few sick people and healed them. And he marveled because of their unbelief (Mk 6: 1–6).

Luke recounts an especially ugly incident. Jesus reproaches his townsmen in their own synagogue for their lack of faith; becoming enraged, "they rose up and put him out of the city, and led him to the brow of the hill on which their city was built, that they might throw him down headlong" (Lk 4: 16–30). Jesus easily eludes them, but the episode tells much about Nazareth and conditions there.

Jesus' public life was likewise hard and painful. We should not romanticize the physical conditions facing an itinerant preacher moving from village to village in the Palestine of those days: heat and cold, hunger and thirst, physical fatigue—these were the daily companions of Jesus and those who accompanied him. The Gospels provide many significant details, almost in passing: Jesus sleeping exhausted in the stern of a boat while a squall on the Lake of Gennesaret terrifies the apostles (Mk 4:37–38); crowds flocking after him in such numbers that he and his followers have no peace, no privacy, no chance to relax, no time even to eat (Mk 6:31); the sparse provisions of the apostles on the occasions of the multiplication of loaves and fishes (Mk 6:38; 8:5). The picture that emerges is one of extreme discomfort, poverty, and physical rigorousness.

But there was far greater suffering than this in Jesus' life. The story told by the Gospels is essentially one of misunderstanding, rejection, harassment, persecution, and ignominious death. Humanly speaking, without reference to faith and to the continuation of his work in and through the community that he founded, the life of Jesus was, as Émile Mersch, S.J., says, "a total failure." Mersch, in his book *The Whole Christ*, tells us:

> Think of it! God Himself becomes flesh for the salvation of men; long years He labors in order to wean them from sin and to draw them to Himself; upon this work He lavishes His prayers, His preaching, His miracles. And what is the result? A few disciples, fearful and hesitant . . . multitudes who, though enthusiastic at times, are ever inconstant, and desert Him when He

turns to serious matters. How far He is from attaining His goal: the conferring of baptism on every creature, the conversion of the whole world!

Many people fail to realize their ambitions and achieve their goals. But in Jesus' case the failure is out of the ordinary. Partly that is because the nature of the ambitions, the goals, and of him who had them in view is so out of the ordinary. But partly also it is because of the nature of the penalty he incurred for so aspiring. He was not simply rejected; the problem was not merely that "they laughed at him" (Mk 5:40) for his claims or that the response even of "many of his disciples" to his solemn promise of the Eucharist was that they "drew back and no longer went about with him" (Jn 6:66). Rather, it was that almost from the start his best efforts provoked deadly hostility. "The Pharisees went out and immediately held counsel with the Herodians against him, how to destroy him" (Mk 3:6). This hostility ultimately led to Jesus' miserable death.

It was a death miserable not only in its physical circumstances but also, as far as we can tell, in its psychological ones: "My God, my God, why hast thou forsaken me?" As Karl Adam says, "Certain as it is that Jesus intended this cry of agony as a Messianic prayer, it is nevertheless the cry of a measureless sense of dereliction."

Why did Jesus have to suffer and die? Was this

necessary or not? Curiously enough, although it was not necessary, it was inevitable.

Because the question is important not only for the light it sheds on Christ's life but also, as we shall see, for the light it sheds on our lives as persons who propose to "follow" (that is, "imitate") him, it is important at the start to set firmly aside certain false notions. For example, it is simply not the case that God the Father punished Jesus for our sins. Yet this is the version of events that sometimes emerges in popular preaching and writing: the Father was enraged by the sins of human beings and was bent on punishing them; the Son, sympathizing with suffering humanity, volunteered to suffer in our stead; the Father, concerned mainly with vengeance, accepted this offer and inflicted a ghastly death on Christ that reduced, although it evidently did not entirely remove, his inclination to smite us also. Now, through some sort of obscure interchange with Jesus (the spiritual equivalent of paying for a train ticket, perhaps?), we can purchase with our prayers, penances, and good works a bit of his propitiatory merit and so ward off damnation, although nothing apparently can be done to stop God from giving us a considerable amount of punishment in this world and probably also in the next (that is, in Purgatory). Caricature though this account may be, is it so very far removed from the way in which these matters have sometimes been presented?

It is true that Jesus in his life, and especially in his Passion and death, both "took on" human sinfulness and "canceled out" sins. "He, though in-nocent," the Holy Father tells us, "takes upon him-self the sufferings of all people, because he takes upon himself the sins of all: . . . It can be said that this is 'substitutive' suffering; but above all it is 'redemptive.' "

The profound truth expressed by the author of the letter to the Hebrews—"Christ was offered up once to take away the sins of many" (Heb 9:28)—stands at the heart of Christianity. But this truth must not be reduced to a dreadful caricature in which the Father is depicted as a bloodthirsty ty-rant; the merit of the redemption lies mainly in the frightfulness of Jesus' suffering, and our prospects of salvation seem to depend on our ability to inter-pose Jesus between us and God. Such a notion of redemption does justice neither to the parties in-volved nor to the reality of the process.

To begin with, it was *not* in itself necessary that Jesus Christ suffer and die in order for us to be redeemed. "The moral value of Christ's human ac-tions," Columba Marmion remarks, repeating what has often been said on the subject, "is measured by the infinite dignity of the Divine Person in whom the human nature subsists and acts." Any human act of Jesus would have sufficed to redeem us if he intended it to have that effect. He need not have endured the scourging, the crowning, the torment of Calvary in order to rescue us from sin.

On the other hand, this line of thinking should not be pushed so far as to divorce Jesus' Passion and death from our redemption, as if what happened to him were the result of a miscalculation on his part, he having already achieved what he set out to do. Not merely historically but morally Christ's suffering and our redemption are intimately linked. "Precisely by means of his Cross," Pope John Paul writes, "he must strike at the roots of evil, planted in the history of man and in human souls. Precisely by means of his Cross he must accomplish *the work of salvation*." It was *not* essential that Jesus suffer and die in order to redeem us, yet his suffering and death are inseparably linked to redemption. How this is so is clear enough when we consider his career.

Presenting himself as a messiah on a model sharply at odds with the expectations of the religious leaders of his time, Jesus came into increasingly bitter conflict with them. Quite soon, it appears, this conflict had become both radicalized—inaccessible to a peaceful solution—and deadly.

The issue that, above all, draws the line between Jesus and his adversaries is observance of the sabbath. In violating the sabbath laws, Jesus affirms that he enjoys authority over both man-made laws and the sabbath itself. This is particularly the case when he performs a miracle of healing on the sabbath in contravention of the law: in such a case there is clearly no logical middle ground—one must either accept his claim to authority or commit oneself to doing away with him. Jesus' enemies choose the latter course.

In sum, "Jesus was ready to suffer death if necessary," writes Germain Grisez, "and his adversaries were ready to kill him if necessary." In due course Jesus' mission, pursued in love and fidelity, led him to go up to Jerusalem in circumstances pointing to the likelihood of his death. The Gospels emphasize both his awareness of the situation and his determination to proceed. He tells his disciples, "Behold, we are going up to Jerusalem; and the Son of man will be delivered to the chief priests and the scribes, and they will condemn him to death, and deliver him to the Gentiles; and they will mock him, and spit upon him, and scourge him, and kill him" (Mk 10: 33–34). He did not turn back. Says Grisez:

> He went to Jerusalem for the last time knowing he would be killed. He could have remained away or, as the hostility grew intense, escaped before disaster befell him. Sooner or later, however, he had either to give up his work and go into hiding, protect himself by miraculous acts, or accept being killed. The first would have betrayed his vocation. The second would have nullified the point of the Incarnation. . . . Thus, only the acceptance of death remains as an option compatible with Jesus' faithfulness to his personal vocation.

It is in this sense that we may reasonably speak of the necessity or inevitability of Jesus' suffering and death: given his task, given the nature of the opposition facing him, and given, finally and most importantly, his absolute, unwavering fidelity to his vocation, these things *had* to happen.

There is, however, another more mysterious perspective from which we must address these matters. It concerns the fact that the Son of God, wishing to enter fully into human experience through his Incarnation, excluded from this neither suffering nor, startling as it may seem, something of the experience of one who sins, even though he committed no sin himself. As part of his redemptive act he took upon himself physical pain and the subjective desolation of the state of sin. We face the heart of this mystery in a statement of St. Paul: "For our sake he made him to be sin who knew no sin, so that in him we might become the righteousness of God" (2 Cor 5:21).

What did it mean for Jesus to "be sin"? He committed no sin. But he did take on all the consequences of sin and experienced them as fully as one human being can—physical and mental agony, the guilty sense of alienation and estrangement from other persons and from God that comes with sin, and, ultimately, an experience of utter desolation.

Why did Jesus take on the consequences of sin? Because suffering is an experience, so that, as Jürgen Moltmann remarks, "suffering must be borne if it is to be overcome." Pope John Paul writes: "Behold, he, though innocent, takes upon himself the sufferings of all people, because he takes upon himself the sins of all. 'The Lord has laid on him the iniquity of us all' [Is 53:6]: *all* human sin in its breadth and depth becomes the true cause of the Redeemer's suffering." There is nothing in life more difficult to understand and accept than the suffering of the innocent. In Jesus Christ it is precisely this experience of innocent suffering that is appropriated and transformed to serve the purposes of redemption.

But it is the love of Jesus, not the suffering as such, that gives this experience its unique value. In freely choosing to lay down his life, Jesus expresses a love and obedience that deserve (that is, merit) the Father's response; he also expresses love for us, which deserves our gratitude and the loyal response of following him. Jesus' love and his suffering are inseparable. Love grows and is transformed through the living out of a commitment; one simply cannot have mature human love apart from the toil and suffering involved in loving service to those who are loved. This is true in Jesus' case, and it is true in ours.

"Upon him was the chastisement that makes us whole, and with his stripes we are healed" (Is 53:5). How is this? How does it happen that what was done by Jesus redeems us? One way of answering is to view the Redemption as essentially a two-sided transaction between Jesus and the Father. It goes like this: we have incurred a debt to God (the punishment due to sin); Christ offers to pay our debt for us, and the Father accepts; Jesus lives, suffers, dies, and the debt is paid—we are redeemed. The sign of this, the incontrovertible evidence that the Father has accepted Jesus' payment as canceling humanity's debt, is the Resurrection.

Although such an explanation is by no means all wrong, the economic metaphor (debt-payment) can obscure the reality (sin-reconciliation) if it is pushed too far. And this explanation has other deficiencies besides. One is that it says nothing about the revelatory character of Jesus' life. All that he said and did is a revelation of God; and this is true also of his suffering.

Pope John Paul II suggests what that might mean in a passage in his 1986 encyclical on the Holy Spirit, *Dominum et vivificantem*. Although the concept of God certainly "excludes from God any pain deriving from deficiencies or wounds," still Scripture itself speaks of God as pained by man's sin—it tells us of "a Father who feels compassion for man, as though sharing his pain." And it is "this inscrutable and indescribable fatherly 'pain'" that brings about, above all, "the wonderful economy of redemptive love in Jesus Christ." From this perspective one might say that, as Jesus' whole life is revelatory of God, so in his suffering he reveals what sin does to God.

It is also important, in giving an account of redemption and Jesus' suffering, not to leave *us* out of the picture or to reduce us to the role of mere bystanders during a transaction between Jesus and the Father. At its worst, such an account suggests that we have no real connection with Jesus' redeeming act. We are passive spectators of our own redemption; we have been redeemed, but we have had nothing to do with it.

In a profound sense, of course, that is true. Redemption is the Father's work in Jesus, and it is Jesus' act, not ours. The grace of our redemption is grace won for us by his living and dying, not by anything we have done or can do. Yet, true as that is, the reality of the situation is also more complex. To respect this complexity, we must consider two concepts that establish a dynamic linkage between us and our redemption. One is solidarity with Christ; the other is co-redemption.

Solidarity with another can be of several kinds, but the solidarity we enjoy—or are at least capable of enjoying—with Jesus Christ is unique. I shall have a great deal to say about this later. For the moment, let these words of Émile Mersch regarding our Savior suffice:

> He is the Head, we are the members; He is the Vine, we are the branches; He is life in its source, and we are animated by that life; He is Unity, and we many are one in Him who is One. Between Him and ourselves all is common. The excellences that He possesses are extended even to us; in Him they exist in their plenitude, whereas they come to us by participation.... His birth and His life, His death and His resurrection—especially His death and resurrection—are also our own, since He is ours; they are prolonged in a mysterious way, by the sacraments and by grace, in our regeneration, in our death to sin, in our elevation to glory.

If this is true, it is an extraordinary fact, with

awesome implications for the way we understand and live our lives. We are one with Jesus Christ, and in him we are one with one another. True, this is a human relationship, but it is also more than that—a sharing in the divine life and also in Jesus' own glorious bodily life. The unity between us and Christ is qualitatively different from any other because it extends to a different order of reality.

As to co-redemption, it is rooted in the reality being described here. Co-redemption has two complementary aspects: first, that because of our unique solidarity with Christ, we participate in and, in a sense, even contribute to our redemption (always bearing in mind that ultimately it is Christ who redeems us, not we who redeem ourselves); second, that we also are empowered by our unity with Jesus to continue his redemptive work, in his name and on his behalf, serving, one might say, as agents of the redemption won by Jesus Christ in our contacts with other human beings.

It is in this context that suffering has its highest meaning, provided one adopts toward it the "evangelical outlook" urged by Pope John Paul II:

> The sufferings of Christ created the good of the world's redemption. This good in itself is inexhaustible and infinite. No man can add anything to it. But at the same time, in the mystery of the Church as his Body, Christ has in a sense opened his own redemptive suffering to all human suffering. In so far as man becomes a sharer in Christ's sufferings—in any part of the world and at any time in history—to that extent he *in his*

own way completes the suffering through which Christ accomplished the Redemption of the world.

But, once again, we are getting ahead of our story. So far, we have considered the role that suffering has in the teaching of Christ and the role it occupied in his own life. There is one other aspect we need briefly to examine: how others responded to Jesus' teaching and especially to his experience.

To say the responses were varied is an understatement. We read in the New Testament of reactions to our Lord's Passion ranging from conversion—Peter—to despair—Judas. No more than anything else about Jesus did his doctrine and personal witness concerning suffering elicit easy, spontaneous acceptance.

Even Mary gradually had to learn her Son's doctrine concerning the redemptive value of suffering. Finally, of course, she did: "Standing by the cross of Jesus [was] his mother" (Jn 19:25). Even in her grief she continued to contemplate the mystery of evil and Jesus' solution to it with attention and deepening comprehension. Moreover, rather than attempting to distance herself from the ugly reality of Jesus' suffering, she appreciated the fact that her vocation involved a call to participate as fully as possible in her Son's Passion and death. At the Annunciation, the Holy Father points out, Mary received a calling "to share, in a singular and unrepeatable way, in the very mission of her Son," and so "her ascent of Calvary and her standing at the foot of the cross together with the Beloved Disciple were a special sort of sharing in the redeeming death of her Son."

Peter and Judas are interesting cases with whom, at least initially, most of us are likely to feel we have more in common than we do with Mary. In both men, human weakness confronts the abysmal reality of the death of Jesus. But where Judas's response is total collapse, withdrawal in horror, and the ultimate, despairing flight of self-destruction, in Peter's case an apparently no less total collapse leads somehow to contrition and a renewed commitment.

The Gospels do not tell enough about either man for us to be able to say with certainty why each acted as he did. That is usually the case with the Gospels. Their very sketchiness about motivation obliges us to consult our own knowledge of why *we* act as we do. What would I have done in Judas's place or Peter's place? Addressing that question can be a sobering experience, something like examining a snapshot of yourself taken when you weren't looking.

Whatever else it signifies, the collapse of Judas is the culmination of his loss of faith in Christ as Redeemer. It seems unlikely that this loss of faith was a sudden, all-in-an-instant thing: probably it took place gradually, over a period of time. What may its stages have been?

The sixth chapter of John's Gospel tells of a great crisis in the public life of Christ. Curiously enough, the crisis occurs just after one of his most striking miracles, the multiplication of the loaves. Awestruck, the crowd pursues Jesus and, catching up with him, asks what other sign he will perform for them. "Our ancestors ate the manna in the wilderness," they point out hopefully. In reply Jesus promises them something greater than manna: the bread of Heaven. "Lord, give us this bread always," the crowd implores. And he answers, "I am the bread of life. He who comes to me shall not hunger, and he who believes in me shall never thirst" (Jn 6: 30–35).

The exchange continues at some length—Jesus becoming more and more explicit, the crowd growing more incredulous and indignant. At last Christ cries out, "Truly, truly, I say to you, unless you eat the flesh of the Son of man and drink his blood, you have no life in you. . . . For my flesh is food indeed, and my blood is drink indeed" (Jn 6: 53, 55).

The effect of this eucharistic discourse was devastating: disbelief not only on the part of the fickle multitude but, it seems, also among no small number of Jesus' followers. "After this many of his disciples drew back and no longer went about with him" (Jn 6:66). And Jesus tells even the Twelve: "One of you is a devil." "He spoke," the Gospel adds, "of Judas" (Jn 6: 70–71).

It is easy to believe that Judas, although he did not outwardly abandon Jesus at this juncture, nevertheless abandoned him in his heart. This is not the Christ to whom he had thought he was committing himself; wild promises about being "the bread of life"—probably ravings, as far as Judas was concerned—fall disastrously short of the brilliant expectations raised by the early miracles that had attracted him. A practical man—treasurer among the apostles—he had hoped that he was allying himself with the Messiah, Israel's liberator from Roman hegemony; but now Judas sees Jesus as a kind of mystical madman, favored with extraordinary powers, to be sure, but, as his delusions grow, increasingly isolated.

Worst of all is the evidence that Jesus himself sees what is happening yet somehow considers the outcome inevitable, necessary. He takes to calling defeat, suffering, and death the fulfillment of his mission and begins to intimate that the same fate awaits his followers. "Evidently," Judas must have reasoned, "the authorities have been right all along: to the extent that anyone takes him seriously—and some, of course, still do—this man is a menace. A decent person would only be doing his duty by helping to put an end to this dangerous charade."

But why, having betrayed Jesus on the basis of some such reasoning, does Judas then despair and end by killing himself? That too is not difficult to imagine.

Whoever Jesus might have been and whatever he might have done, he did not deserve to die that kind of death. He, Judas, had contributed to a massive and brutal miscarriage of justice. But now it was too late to do anything about it—too late both for Jesus and for him. Jesus was dying, dead; his extravagant claims to be a source of life for others manifestly had been exploded. As for Judas, his role in sending this deluded but high-minded eccentric to his death was inexcusable: Jesus had befriended him, taken him into his inner circle, trusted him. Judas could see no possibility of pardon for a man who had betrayed such trust; Jesus' death thus sealed Judas's fate.

For Judas, of course, regarded it as simply that—a death: final, definitive, the ultimate destruction of hope and confirmation of despair—and he responded accordingly. Repentance and reconciliation were out of the question, since he had already rejected the idea that Jesus opens up any such possibilities to his followers, and he had found support for his views in Christ's Passion and death. Rejection of the whole redemptive meaning of Jesus' ministry brought Judas to this point. All that remained open to him was grief's perversion: despair.

What of Peter? Where did he go wrong, and why did he not also end as Judas did?

Peter, much like Judas, approached the Passion with a too limited notion of Jesus' mission. He looked for a messiah who would be a new King David, not a suffering redeemer. "And Jesus said to them, 'You will all fall away; for it is written, "I will strike the shepherd, and the sheep will be scattered"'" (Mk 14:27). Peter's reply, sincerely intended but full of bravado, was, "Even though they all fall away, I will not." Jesus answered, "Truly, I say to you, this very night, before the cock crows twice, you will deny me three times." But Peter kept insisting—"vehemently," Mark tells us—"If I must die with you, I will not deny you" (Mk 14: 29–31).

Peter's downfall had been marked out much earlier, long before those fateful few hours between the Last Supper and Christ's condemnation to death. It was signaled precisely at the moment when he challenged the idea that Christ's way was a way of suffering. That incident, the Gospels suggest, occurred not long before Jesus began his last trip to Jerusalem.

By then the tide had already begun clearly to turn against Jesus. His enemies were mobilized, his popularity was on the wane. The crowds were still there, sometimes at least, but with perhaps more the morbid attitude of people awaiting the outcome of a tragic spectacle than the hopeful attitude of people anticipating the liberation of Israel. Keenly aware of what was happening, Jesus took steps to prepare and strengthen those who were still loyal to him.

The first step in this urgent program was to deepen their faith. On the way to the neighborhood of Caesarea Philippi, "Jesus asked his disciples, 'Who do men say that I am?'" There was a hodgepodge of answers, including "John the Baptist" and "one of the prophets." Then Jesus confronted them squarely: "But who do you say that I am?" Peter, habitually the first to speak, gave the answer: "You are the Christ!" (Mk 8: 27–29).

As it turned out, this response proved to be Peter's salvation. But how, we may reasonably ask, could a man who had confessed Jesus to be the Christ, the Messiah, find himself so soon in the position of denying him and abandoning him? (And how, we may just as well ask, can we who confidently assert our faith in Christ find ourselves so often in much the same position?) In Peter's case (and ours, too?) the answer concerned an inability to accept the role of suffering in the life of Christ the Messiah and in the lives of those who wish to follow him. Peter believed that evil could be overcome by overpowering it; he had yet to learn that, in God's plan, evil is overcome by being experienced, that is, by undergoing suffering and being healed by divine power.

Peter's profession of faith triggered in Jesus what must have struck the disciples as a strange and frightening reaction. Instead of embracing the title of Messiah and inaugurating a new and more glorious phase in his ministry, he commenced speaking of dark and terrifying things. "He began to teach them that the Son of Man must suffer many things, and be rejected by the elders and the chief priests and the scribes, and be killed, and after three days rise again." This is too much for Peter, who "took him and began to rebuke him." We can easily imagine the scenario: "You're making things too hard on yourself, Lord, and on us, too. Use your miraculous power to get the best of your enemies! You can be crowned and sitting in David's chair next week.

Surely that makes more sense than this talk about suffering?" Peter and the rest looked for a messiah who would be Israel's political liberator and bring about peace and prosperity in this world; God's kingdom—not of this world—is not yet part of their thinking.

Jesus' reaction was astonishing: he rebuked Peter as harshly as he has ever rebuked anyone or ever will; calling Peter a devil, he told him to get out of his sight, because Peter was concerned not with God's ends but with men's (Mk 8: 31–33).

Jesus was telling Peter that he, like Satan, was in opposition to the will of God. In continuing, in effect, the mysterious episode of temptation at the very beginning of Jesus' public life, Peter was proposing that Jesus be messiah according to a human model, the way of worldly victory, rather than the divine plan, the way of redemptive suffering. It is not that Peter suggested that Jesus engage in gross self-indulgence or even that he withdraw from public life. Peter merely expressed what any of us would: a reasonable distaste for suffering and an understandable preference for visible, tangible, immediate success. As Jürgen Moltmann says, "Peter wants what all men want. . . . We want to achieve. We want to be immune from frustration, suffering and contempt. . . . It is only power which impresses. It is only success which succeeds."

But Jesus says no; it is necessary that he suffer, so that he may accomplish what he came to do. The way of power and worldly victory will not do, Jesus tells us, for they cannot overcome what cannot be destroyed—evil as privation. His approach to evil is to heal it. To do this he must come to grips with suffering and death, so that they also will have their places in God's redemptive plan.

What, then, saved Peter and kept him from ending as Judas did? An answer is implicit in his acceptance of Jesus as Messiah. It is his faith, as personal loyalty to Jesus. At the start Peter did not fully comprehend the implications of his commitment of faith; just as we hardly understand ours. Later, under pressure, cowardice led him to fail miserably in facing up to the demands of his vocation; so it is with us in our ways. But, even though Peter's courage failed him, his faith in Jesus, his essential loyalty, did not waver. Consequently, Peter was able to assent to Jesus' conviction (even if he could not understand it) that suffering was necessary to the fulfillment of his ministry and, later, to Peter's discipleship. Thus, where Judas may have shed sterile tears of despair, Peter shed tears of true contrition.

Peter and Judas are major figures in the drama of the Gospels. There is another, however, who occupies a comparatively obscure place in that story, yet whose behavior raises a question worth pondering in relation to the matters under consideration here. I mean Nicodemus.

His appearances in the Gospel of St. John are in startling contrast with one another. We are introduced to "a man of the Pharisees, named Nicodemus, a ruler of the Jews" (Jn 3:1)—in other words, a personage of substance, respectability, and even power, a prominent figure in the social and religious establishment of the day, a well-accepted member of the club. It is reported of Nicodemus that he "came to him [Jesus] by night" (Jn 3:2). This small detail is important, for the author refers to it again much later, on the occasion of Nicodemus's last appearance in the Gospel: "Nicodemus, who had at first come to [Jesus] by night" (Jn 19:39).

The point seems clear enough. We are meant to understand that this respectable man was afraid to be known as a follower or even as a sympathizer of Jesus. This is hardly surprising. At no time did the social and religious establishment find Jesus congenial; the conflict that was to end in Jesus' death began early in his public life and continued to the end. Merely in approaching Jesus, Nicodemus risked the criticism and disapproval of his peers. Caution dictated that he approach this controversial but oddly compelling itinerant preacher "by night."

Such caution makes perfectly good sense; yet it seems inconsistent with the role Nicodemus plays in his two other appearances in John's Gospel. The first of these is related in the seventh chapter. The leaders of the people are conspiring against Jesus. Nicodemus speaks up: "Does our law judge a man without first giving him a hearing and learning what he does?" (Jn 7:51). A reasonable question but a surprisingly bold one for a cautious man in these circumstances. Then, following the crucifix-

ion, it is this same cautious member of the establishment who joins Joseph of Arimathea in seeing to
Jesus' burial. "Nicodemus also, who had at first
come to him by night, came bringing a mixture of
myrrh and aloes, about a hundred pounds' weight"
(Jn 19:39).

These inconsistencies are difficult to understand.
If this careful man was too apprehensive to risk
public identification with Jesus at a time when he
was popular and successful—a time when Nicodemus might have calculated that a modest investment of personal prestige in Jesus could perhaps
pay handsome dividends in the long run—if, in
short, even at the crest of Jesus' career Nicodemus
was too frightened to approach Jesus openly, how is
it that he could step forward at the end of the story,
when Jesus had been shown to be, as Nicodemus's
colleagues had alleged, a troublemaker who would
come to no good end? The game was up; Jesus had
died; the disciples, terrified, had scattered; the
whole miserable charade was finished. And then
Nicodemus, the worthy personage who in the heady
days of Christ's popularity would not chance an
open display of sympathy, emerged from the shad-
ows bearing his myrrh and aloes and risking his
reputation, his social standing, and possibly even
more, to attend to the burial of this calamitous
failure. Why?

The answer is suggested in Nicodemus's first appearance in the Gospel, where John tells us something of central importance, something crucial not

only to comprehending Nicodemus's behavior but to understanding our solidarity with Jesus and so finding the meaning in our suffering. The answer concerns baptism.

The dialogue between Jesus and Nicodemus in the following paragraphs is like several in John's Gospel (Jn 3:1–21): someone approaches Christ with a naïve question; Jesus gives an answer that at first seems unrelated to what has been asked but in fact invites the questioner to go deeper than he ever dreamed; and the ensuing conversation proceeds through a kind of dialectic of misunderstanding and renewed insistence, as the interlocutor's bewilderment gradually falls away beneath the hammer blows of Jesus' teaching.

Nicodemus came seeking a clear statement concerning Jesus' identity. No doubt the Pharisee had his own suspicions, but he wanted to hear what Jesus had to say. "Rabbi," he therefore commenced courteously, "we know you are a teacher come from God; for no one can do these signs that you do, unless God is with him."

And Jesus replied, "Truly, truly, I say to you, unless one is born anew, he cannot see the kingdom of God." He had discerned the seeds of something promising in Nicodemus; he was bent on carrying this man further than the Pharisee expected.

Understandably, however, Nicodemus was skeptical: "How can a man be born when he is old? Can he enter a second time into his mother's womb and be born?" Jesus answered with what we now take as a concise statement concerning the purpose and effect of baptism: "Truly, truly, I say to you, unless one is born of water and the Spirit, he cannot enter the kingdom of God. That which is born of the flesh is flesh, and that which is born of the Spirit is spirit. Do not marvel that I said to you, 'You must be born anew.'"

The Pharisee was dumbfounded: "How can this be?" Jesus' reply was an ironic rebuke: "Are you a teacher of Israel, and yet you do not understand this?" (Some Pharisees, of course, were not shy about claiming to understand and pass judgment on virtually every matter of religious belief and moral practice; Jesus' words seem aimed at their pretensions, as well as at Nicodemus as typical.) Then, suddenly, the tone changes, and we are plunged into one of those passages whose sublimity is peculiar to John among the evangelists:

> As Moses lifted up the serpent in the wilderness, so must the Son of man be lifted up, that whoever believes in him may have eternal life.
>
> For God so loved the world that he gave his only Son, that whoever believes in him should not perish but have eternal life. For God sent the Son into the world, not to condemn the world, but that the world might be saved through him (Jn 3: 14–17).

Jesus speaks here of his redemptive mission, referring clearly to the distinctive means by which he will complete his work: his "lifting up" on the cross of Calvary. At the same time, he affirms that solidarity with him is necessary for salvation; those who believe in him will have "eternal life."

How is this solidarity to be achieved? The answer is implicit in the very context of this passage: through baptism. Immediately preceding the affirmation that union with Jesus is indispensable to salvation is his doctrine on baptism; immediately following is the information, found only in John's Gospel, that Jesus carried on a public baptismal ministry (Jn 3:22). These few verses link crucial themes: baptism, union with Jesus, Christ's redemptive mission, our sharing in the Redemption, and the suffering of the cross. John is saying that these things constitute a single dynamic process that lies at the very heart of Christian life—which, in fact, *is* Christian life.

To understand this process better, we need to turn from John's Gospel to St. Paul. As clearly and distinctly as possible, Paul teaches that baptism is the sacrament of our incorporation into Jesus Christ. This concept—incorporation into Christ—is difficult, mysterious. Much of the rest of this book will be spent exploring its meaning and seeking to relate it to our experience of suffering. But its relevance for Paul is overwhelming, urgent; and its reality begins in baptism.

> Do you not know that all of us who have been baptized into Christ Jesus were baptized into his death? We were buried therefore with him by baptism into death, so that, as Christ was raised

from the dead by the glory of the Father, we too
might walk in newness of life. . . . But if we have
died with Christ, we believe that we shall also live
with him. . . . So you also must consider your-
selves dead to sin and alive to God in Christ
Jesus" (Rom 6:3–4, 8, 11).

Baptism is not a sacrament to which most people
pay a great deal of attention. If pressed, most would
probably say it makes those who receive it members
of the Christian community, the Church; some
might add that it takes away original sin. These
things are true, but the full reality of baptism is vastly
more exciting than such dry formulas express.

Baptism is the commencement of a *new life*—life
"with" and "in" Jesus Christ. By nature we are in
solidarity with Adam and the sin of Adam; by baptism we enter into a new and supernatural union
with Christ and his life. We become Christ's "members" in a corporate entity to which, following Paul,
we give the name "the Mystical Body of Christ."

And in this new context we find, specifically, the
meaning of our suffering. "In this Body," Pope John
Paul II says, "Christ wishes to be united with every
individual, and in a special way he is united with
those who suffer. . . . In the mystery of the Church
as his Body, Christ has in a sense opened his own
redemptive suffering to all human suffering."

All this may seem far removed from Nicodemus,
too timid at first to approach Christ except secretly,
yet later, when all has ended in apparent failure and
others have fled, willing to declare himself by a bold

gesture a follower of the crucified Jesus. But I have not forgotten Nicodemus; I have only been trying to understand him. Now we know enough to make an educated guess about the dramatic change that took place in him.

We know, first of all, that Jesus opened the Pharisee's eyes to the reality of baptism. Either then or later, it seems reasonable to suppose, Nicodemus shared, in deed or by desire, in baptism's spiritual benefits and became a committed follower of Christ. And more than that: he received the grace, given only to Mary, John, and a few others, to confront the event of Calvary without flinching or surrendering to despair.

Nicodemus did not know, on that Good Friday, that Jesus would rise on Easter, but he seems to have known that Jesus' Passion and death somehow were appropriate and necessary elements in his mission as Messiah. More than that, he had glimpsed how suffering and death fit into the life of one who wishes to follow Christ. That insight gave him courage.

Pope John Paul remarks that, in Jesus' first conversation with Nicodemus, he introduced the timid Pharisee "into the very heart of God's salvific work." And in the mystery of baptism, by which we become one with Jesus Christ and begin to share in a new life that is the life of God, we also are introduced into God's redemptive activity and into our own participation in redemption through, among other things, suffering.

III

Union with Christ

Near the beginning of his apostolic exhortation on suffering, Pope John Paul II writes: "These words seem to be found at the end of the long road that winds through the suffering which forms part of the history of man and which is illuminated by the word of God. These words have as it were the value of a final discovery, which is accompanied by joy." The "words" that the Holy Father contends so remarkably unlock the riddle of suffering are those from St. Paul that we have already quoted: "In my flesh I complete what is lacking in Christ's afflictions for the sake of his body, that is, the church" (Col 1:24). Here, the Holy Father maintains, we find "the final stage of the spiritual journey in relation to suffering."

This is strange. At first St. Paul's words seem neither very clear nor very satisfying—one of those mystifying bits of Pauline rhetoric in which, the reader may suspect, the writer's enthusiasm has moved him to pious exaggeration. "Even now," Paul writes, just before the passage singled out by the Pope, "I rejoice in my sufferings for your sake" (Col 1:24). One nods, smiles a little: How like Paul!

That is a mistake. No single short passage from Colossians, nor, indeed, any other single passage from the New Testament or any other source, by itself explains the Christian meaning of suffering. But even so, Paul's words merit the description given them by the Pope: "a final discovery." We have here a definitive statement of the role suffering is meant to play in the life of a follower of Jesus: "In my flesh I complete what is lacking in Christ's afflictions for the sake of his body, that is, the church." It is essential to understand what this statement means.

A Christian no longer lives his life—or is at least no longer *meant* to live his life—in isolation. By baptism he is incorporated into Christ, made a member of Christ's Mystical Body. But this is a "membership" unlike any other. One who is a member of the Mystical Body is united with Christ, shares Christ's life, participates in Christ's human acts and merit; through the Eucharist Jesus lives in him, and he in Jesus. The union between Christ and the member is not merely moral, a bond between leader and follower; it is, as one writer expresses it, "real" and "ontological." These words signify a union, a sharing of life, that exceeds every other relationship in our experience to the point that a member of Christ can speak of Christ as his very identity.

Moreover, membership in the Mystical Body of Christ also signifies a unique and unparalleled solidarity among the members of the Body themselves. We are one Body; what we do directly and immediately affects the other members. We are linked by grace, so that our every action contributes either to the spiritual benefit of the others and the edification (that is, the building up) of the entire Body or else to their spiritual detriment and to the tearing down of the Body.

Suffering, St. Paul says, plays a special role in this scheme. The suffering of a Christian is at once a kind of replication—a reliving—of the suffering of Christ and a form of participation in the Passion and death of Jesus. At the same time, suffering is the application by the individual of these episodes in Jesus' life to the unique circumstances of his or her own life: "In my flesh I complete what is lacking in Christ's afflictions"; but more than that: "for the sake of his body, that is, the church."

As with the suffering of Jesus, so with the suffering of the Christian, this dismal experience has meaning and merit: it benefits others, it builds up the Mystical Body. By participating through our suffering in the suffering of Jesus, we become co-redeemers with him.

"You will suffer," St. Augustine says, "just so much as must be added of your sufferings to the complete Passion of Christ, who suffered as our Head and who continues still to suffer in His members, that is, in us. Into this common treasury each pays what he owes, and according to each one's ability we all contribute our share of suffering. The full measure of the Passion will not be attained until the end of the world." Dom Columba Marmion, reflecting on both Paul and Augustine, says:

To understand the mystery of Christ, we must
not separate Him from His mystical body. Christ
is not the "whole Christ," according to the expression of the great Doctor, unless He is taken
as *united* to the Church. He is the Head of the
Church which forms his mystical body. Hence,
since Christ has brought His share of expiation,
it remains for the mystical body to bring its
share. . . . [God has] determined a share of sufferings for the Church to distribute among her
members. Thereby each of them is to cooperate
in the expiation of one's own faults, or in the
expiation endured, after the example of the Divine Master, for the faults of others.

This is a breathtaking vision of Christian life and
of suffering's role in it. "I have been crucified with
Christ," Paul announces, "it is no longer I who live,
but Christ who lives in me" (Gal 2:20)—and suddenly we recognize that we also are meant to say the
same. This recognition bursts the boundaries of
tepid Christianity, to encompass an awesome drama
in which, for once, our humdrum lives *matter* because they either succeed or fail in being individual-
ized reenactments of the redemptive life of Jesus
Christ.

But this vision *is* hard to take in. We need to retrace
our steps and reexamine some of these ideas in
more leisurely fashion. Perhaps the best place to
begin is with the idea of the "following," or "imitation," of Christ.

It is an old idea, familiar to readers of Thomas à

Kempis and many other spiritual writers, but it goes back even farther, to the New Testament itself. Jesus instructs his disciples to take up their crosses and follow *him*—to lose their very lives for *his* sake. "A disciple is not above his teacher," he explains. "It is enough for the disciple to be like his teacher" (Mt 9:24–25). St. Paul seems consumed with the idea that he, a follower of Jesus Christ, is to be like Christ. "And we all, with unveiled face, beholding the glory of the Lord, are being changed into his likeness" (2 Cor 3:18).

In one sense there is nothing unusual or difficult to understand about this. Consciously or unconsciously, we are continually modeling our behavior on the behavior of others. An enormous amount of what we do, from table manners to work, is based on observing others and trying to act like them.

To some extent, the imitation of Christ is like this—a more or less conscious and deliberate imitation of Christ's behavior. We read about Jesus in the New Testament and other books; we hear sermons about him; we may see films that depict his life; and, if we are sufficiently impressed, we reflect on what we've read and heard and seen and then attempt to apply those lessons to our own conduct. This is a reasonable, valid, and commendable way of "imitating" Christ.

Still, it is difficult to read the New Testament even casually without receiving the impression that the imitation of Christ also signifies something more radical than this. Consider Jesus' words in one of his eucharistic discourses in John's Gospel: "Unless you eat the flesh of the Son of man and drink his blood, you have no life in you" (Jn 6:54). This might, of course, be merely figurative language; yet it *sounds* starkly literal; not only that, John tells us that it led to Jesus' rejection even by many of his disciples. A mere figure of speech, easily understandable as such, would hardly have had that effect or, if it had, one might have expected Jesus to clear up the misunderstanding. That he did not suggests that in taking him literally the disbelieving disciples understood him correctly.

Or consider Paul. He is an extreme case.

> We are afflicted in every way... but not driven to despair.... Always carrying in the body the death of Jesus, so that the life of Jesus may be manifested in our mortal flesh (2 Cor 4:8, 10).

> For I through the law died to the law, that I might live to God. I have been crucified with Christ; it is no longer I who live, but Christ who lives in me (Gal 2:19–20).

> We are members of his body... and the two shall become one (Eph 5:30).

> For to me to live is Christ, and to die is gain (Phil 1:21).

Paul even wants us to share this reality: "My little children, with whom I am again in travail until Christ be formed in you" (Gal 4:19).

Examples can be multiplied, but the point is clear: we are dealing here with a relationship that, although it can be described as the "imitation" of Christ, goes far beyond the ordinary human experience of imitating someone. It is a relationship of incomparably intimate and complete union: we live in Christ, he in us. The reality is best expressed by metaphors: we are members of Christ's body; he is a vine, we are branches. However expressed, the relationship between us and Jesus goes beyond any other in our experience.

Different writers make this point variously. Émile Mersch observes that the relationship between Christ and the Christian can be understood in two ways, "both good, and both orthodox." One way refers to "a reality of the moral order." In his book *The Whole Christ*, Mersch says:

> According to this view, all can be explained by the fact of our resemblance to Christ and our absolute and manifold dependence upon Him. The Lord is the model of all our virtues, the principle of all our hopes, the expiation of all our sins, the source of all our supernatural life. . . . In a word, we are joined to Him by all the bonds that can attach one man to another; and here these bonds are far more numerous and far more powerful.

The second view, "characterized by its realism and its mysticism," Mersch presents in this way:

> Its great and guiding principle is to take the full and complete meaning of the Scriptural and patristic statements. According to this view, men have a true union with Christ, a real and onto-

94

logical union; He is really and truly in them and we are in Him; we are really and truly one in Him as He is one with the Father. . . . It is best to retain the traditional name and call it a "mystical" union. However, it must be clearly understood that this term is by no means synonymous with "nebulous" or "semi-real." On the contrary, it specifies something which in plenitude and reality surpasses the things of nature and the positive concepts that our reason can elaborate.

Needless to say, Mersch, theologian of the Mystical Body, understands this second view to be the more correct one.

So do many spiritual writers and mystics. But it is important to understand that the relationship of unity with Christ, which is in question here, is not reserved for those special souls called mystics. It is the same relationship existing more or less perfectly between Jesus and *every* soul living in the state of grace. Perhaps "mysticism" merely signifies a greater than ordinary degree of experiential awareness of this relationship. In any case, Eugene Boylan writes, "The foundation of the whole spiritual life lies in some principle of solidarity between Christ and the sinner." He goes on to say:

When St. Thomas considers this difficulty . . . of the transfer of punishment and merit between Christ and the Christian, he solves it by saying that Christ could do all these things for us because He and we together form "one mystical person." . . . To the question then: "How did Christ save us?" the answer is: "by making us part of Himself." And when we ask: "How are we to save ourselves?" the answer is: "by making ourselves part of Christ."

Regarding this, Caryll Houselander tells us:

> The whole meaning of our Catholic faith is union, union with Christ, and through Him, union with one another. This oneness is not a unity of ideas or ambitions or acts or circumstances, it is not a unity such as one finds in a society or group. . . . It is oneness like the oneness of the various parts of the human body.

In practical terms, she says, the result is that "we, strange as it is, live lives analogous to His."

There are, of course, extremes to be avoided in pursuing this idea of oneness. Let us put firmly aside any notion of being absorbed into God so as to lose identity and individuality. Jesus is Jesus; a Christian is himself. However close the unity between them, they remain two distinct persons. It will never be otherwise.

Perhaps, though, we are more likely to err in the other direction—clinging to individualistic attitudes that keep us from entertaining the possibility of unity with Christ. Especially is this true of the thought that what is involved is a real, bodily unity. "Modern individualism blocks understanding here," remarks Germain Grisez. "We tend to think persons are in all respects units completely separate and isolated from one another." But that is not so. There is, for example, a "dynamic unity" of husband and wife in the generative act; and, in fact, the letter to the Ephesians uses the unity of husband and wife to illustrate the unity of Christ and the Church (Eph 5:22–23). Grisez says, in summary:

> Baptism and the gift of the Spirit forge the bodily unity of Christians with Jesus (1 Cor 12:12–13). The unity is in him, based upon his individual, resurrected body (Rom 12:4–5). Real unity with the bodily death and resurrection of Jesus is brought about in baptism; this bodily unity of the Christian with the individual body of the Lord Jesus makes of the Church a physical whole (Col 1:22; 2:12, 17; 3:1–4, 15). Maintaining this bodily communion depends upon the sacrament of the Eucharist (Jn 6:53–57).

Several things follow naturally from the unity of the Christian with Jesus. One is that Jesus' attributes become the Christian's; what is true of Jesus can also be affirmed of the person who is in solidarity with him. Marmion says: "So His wisdom, His justice, His holiness, His strength have become *our* wisdom, *our* justice, *our* strength. . . . All that He has is *ours*; we are rich with His riches, holy with His holiness."

Furthermore, our lives resemble Jesus' life. Unquestionably, this is a reality to be approached with a certain caution. It is not, after all, as if one were literally reenacting the episodes in the life of Christ, and someone who attempted to do so would not only strike others as eccentric but would be making the effort to no good purpose. This, surely, is not what the "imitation" of Christ means. Yet the idea that the life of the Christian reproduces the life of Christ—that it traces the same patterns in its inner reality even while its external details differ vastly— occurs again and again in the literature. "In the life and death of the Christian," writes Karl Adam, "there is reproduced and manifested in virtue of his baptism the life and death of Christ."

The extraordinary relationship between the Christian and Jesus Christ begins, as we saw earlier, in the sacrament of baptism. What a sadly diminished understanding of baptism many of us have! Years ago, all that most Catholics understood about the sacrament was that it washes away the stain of Original Sin; today, for many people, baptism simply signals one's "reception into the Christian community," or something of that sort.

Both concepts are true, but neither suggests the full and dramatic truth that in baptism we enter into the relationship of unity with Jesus Christ, dying to our old and unredeemed selves, as he died in accomplishing redemption upon Calvary, and rising to a new life, which is participation in divine life, just as he rose with a new, glorified life on Easter.

> Do you not know that all of us who have been baptized into Christ Jesus were baptized into his death? We were buried therefore with him by baptism into death, so that as Christ was raised from the dead by the glory of the Father, we too might walk in newness of life.

> For if we have been united with him in a death
> like his, we shall certainly be united with him in
> a resurrection like his (Rom 6: 3–5).

The fullness of this resurrected life lies for us at some point in the future; yet because of our present bodily unity with the risen Christ, perfected through worthy participation in the Eucharist, we are to some degree living that life, imperfectly but truly, even now. In sum, we can say that to be baptized into Christ does not mean simply to become subject to him or even merely to commit oneself to him; it means being incorporated into him.

The most important principle of union with Christ, first received in baptism, is grace. Aelred Graham, reflecting on the meaning of St. Paul's statement that "we have the mind of Christ" (1 Cor 2:16), remarks that "through grace and charity . . . we ourselves have the first beginning of the 'mind of Christ'; in proportion as they are intensified within us do we become like to Him." He continues:

> Never, of course, can we be so united with God
> as to form one personality with Him; nor, in the
> present life, can we be sustained by the vision of
> the divine essence. But, by way of compensa-
> tion, we are given that creaturely participation
> in the divine nature which is sanctifying grace;
> and, to correspond with Christ's knowledge, we
> receive the supernatural illumination of faith
> and the gifts of wisdom and understanding.
> From these thoughts we are led easily to the
> conclusion that the imitation of Christ consists
> essentially in knowing and loving, in our own

measure, what He knows and loves. From this knowledge and love Christlike action will follow.

This way of putting the matter can be startling to someone who thinks of grace, if he thinks of it at all, only as merit earned for good behavior. The best and most orthodox understanding of grace is that it is our participation in the nature—indeed, in the very life—of God. The life of grace, which is a life of solidarity with Jesus begun in baptism and lived out in the pursuit of ever greater unity with him, is no mere superficial pattern of natural benevolence punctuated by ritualistic religious observances; it is a sharing in divine life.

As many writers have pointed out, the doctrine of incorporation in Christ includes a doctrine of human divinization in Christ. We are to take literally such statements as this from the first letter of John: "If you know that he is righteous, you may be sure that every one who does right is born of him. See what love the Father has given us, that we should be called children of God; and so we are. . . . Beloved, we are God's children now" (1 Jn 2: 29–3: 1–2). Or this, from the first letter of Peter: "You have been born anew, not of perishable seed but of imperishable, through the living and abiding word of God" (1 Pet 1: 23). As the divine and human come together in one person, Jesus Christ, the Son of God by nature, so we, God's human children by adoption, participate in the divine nature by sanctifying grace, which comes to us and increases in us insofar as our lives are lived in unity with Jesus.

Unity with Christ is not merely an individual experience; it has a corporate, communal dimension. Holy Communion, which unites us bodily with the risen Lord, also makes us one fellowship sharing together bodily in his Resurrection-life. This reality, to which we give the name the Mystical Body of Christ, is expressed by St. Paul in a number of places. The heart of his teaching is this: "For as in one body we have many members, and all the members do not have the same function, so we, though many, are one body in Christ, and individually members one of another" (Rom 12:4–5). The principal elements of the doctrine are the unity of the members with Christ, their unity with one another, and their functional diversity—they have different roles to play, different tasks to perform.

Even more difficult to grasp than the notion of our unity with Jesus may be this notion of our unity with one another in and through the Mystical Body. It too goes emphatically against the grain of individualism, the assumption that even—or perhaps especially—in matters of the spirit we are solitary, alone with God. Paul, however, hammers home this element of the doctrine:

> But now in Christ Jesus you who once were far off have been brought near in the blood of Christ. For he is our peace, who has made us both one, and has broken down the dividing wall of hostility, by abolishing in his flesh the law of commandments and ordinances, that he might create in himself one new man in place of the

two, so making peace, and might reconcile us both to God in one body through the cross, thereby bringing the hostility to an end (Eph 2:13–16).

As with our unity with Jesus, so with our unity with one another in the Mystical Body—we may imagine that this doctrine expresses simply a moral solidarity, though one that is unusually intense and deep-seated. But such thinking overlooks the mysterious bodily communion Christians enjoy with Jesus and with one another in the Eucharist. Hence, we must take the doctrine of unity as expressing a reality that exceeds ordinary moral solidarity. Mersch says that all Christians have

> a common life, flowing from the same principle that gives each one his individual life. . . . Each is perfected by all the others in what is most interior to himself, that is, in this Christ from whom he has life; each has his personal life and holiness, his good works and his merits, but he possesses them in common with all other men; they are truly his own, but at the same time truly theirs.

One consequence of this unity is that we are able to assist and benefit one another spiritually. This also can be understood in an unremarkable sense: we can help one another by good example, instruction, works of charity, and so forth. That, of course, is true and important. But the doctrine also signifies what Caryll Houselander meant when she said, "The whole meaning of our Catholic faith is union, union with Christ, and through Him, union with

one another." Likening this union to the oneness of
the various parts of the human body, she adds that
"because this is so, no Christian can be separated
from any other Christian by anything whatever; we
are one with our dead, we are one with our distant
martyrs, we are one with our sinners."

What this means in practice can be illustrated by
a story St. Thérèse of Lisieux tells in her auto-
biography:

> I'd heard of a criminal who had just been con-
> demned to death for some frightful murder. It
> seemed that he would die without repenting. I
> was determined at all costs to save him from
> hell. I used every means I could. I knew that by
> myself I could do nothing, so I offered God the
> infinite merits of our Lord and the treasures of
> the Church. I was quite certain that my prayers
> would be answered, but to give me courage to go
> on praying for sinners I said to God: "I am sure
> You will forgive this wretched Pranzini. I shall
> believe You have done so even if he does not
> confess or give any other sign of repentance, for
> I have complete faith in the infinite mercy of
> Jesus. But I ask You for just one sign of his
> repentance to encourage me."
>
> This prayer was answered. . . . On the day af-
> ter his execution I eagerly opened *La Croix* and I
> had to rush away to hide my tears at what I read.
> Pranzini had mounted the scaffold without con-
> fessing and was ready to thrust his head beneath
> the guillotine's blade when he suddenly turned,
> seized the crucifix offered him by the priest, and
> thrice kissed the Sacred Wounds.
>
> I had been given my sign.

One can, of course, take this as the pious nonsense of a child whose head was filled too full of religious notions at too early an age. But others find it an instance of the "law of spiritual fruitfulness," described by Eugene Boylan: "It is not always the priest who preaches the sermon who is responsible for the conversions produced by it.... Very often the real source of his success is to be found in the prayers and sufferings of some hidden soul"—in this instance, the prayers of St. Thérèse.

We benefit one another in the spiritual order to the extent God chooses to use our good acts as elements in the providential plan according to which he dispenses grace. It is grace that is effective, not what we do, and God does not have to wait for us to act; yet the doctrine of the Mystical Body not only invites but requires us to believe that what we do is important in this context. And St. Thomas Aquinas says:

> Just as in a living body, the operation of one member promotes the welfare of the whole body, so it is in the spiritual (or mystical) body, which is the Church. Since all the faithful are one body, the good of each is communicated to the others ... whence it follows that whoever possesses charity shares in all the good that is done in the whole world.

This body is, of course, the Mystical Body of Christ, one of whose principal functions is to continue and complete Christ's work in history. Quite naturally, then, phenomena associated originally with the actual, historical life of Jesus tend to be mirrored in subsequent ages in the life of Christ's Mystical Body. It is a function of the presence of Jesus himself in this community he brought into being and sustains as the instrumentality of his continued presence in and action upon history.

To be sure, one ought not to press this thought to ludicrous extremes, as if episodes from Jesus' life were in concrete actuality being reenacted. The reality is more nearly as Robert Hugh Benson expresses it—like "the repetition of a chemical experiment." Benson explains it this way:

> If, then, we find the same psychological situations as those recorded in the Gospels continually reproduced under similar circumstances—if we find, that is, Peters and Judases and Pilates swarming round the Church's progress through the ages—if we find that the same comments are made, the same paradoxes generated, the same accusations leveled, the same criticisms, the same bursts of flame and thunder—if we find the lepers healed, the dead raised, the devils cast out, and the same explanations offered of these phenomena by the incredulous—if we find the same amazing claims uttered to the world, and the same repudiations, demurrings, and acceptances of those claims—if, in short, we find . . . the endless intricacies and phenomena recorded in the Gospels reproduced on the stage of human history, the conclusion will be overwhelmingly strong that the same Personality that produced those phenomena then is reproducing them now.

In pursuing the practical implications of these matters we must be careful to avoid confusing metaphors with actuality. The "Mystical Body" is a case in point. It should be clear by now that the expression refers to a profound reality; but the expression itself remains a figure of speech, like the "vine and branches" of John's Gospel, which points to the same reality. It would be a monstrous caricature to suppose that the relationship between Christ and Christians (as well as the relationship among Christians themselves) constituted them an actual, physical body, any more than it makes the relationship an actual, physical vine bearing branches and grapes. These are attempts to express in figurative language a reality of an altogether different order.

Neither should we fall into the pantheistic trap of supposing that unity with Jesus by faith and the Eucharist and divinization by sanctifying grace turn us into particles of God, lacking individuality and personhood. No matter how close the unity, either now or in Heaven, we are not absorbed into God; we do not lose our irreducible uniqueness. Nor, as Mersch remarks, are we to imagine that real, ontological, mystical unity with Jesus means we are "really and absolutely Christ Himself, or . . . fragments or emanations of Christ"; to suppose otherwise would be a kind of " 'panchristism,' quite as contradictory as it is naïve, and fraught with the most absurd consequences."

Still another danger is a quietistic mentality, a sort of false mysticism, according to which the "work" of the interior life is understood as so exclusively God's that the Christian has nothing to do. It is true that all that has merit, all that is worthwhile, all that is efficacious in the interior life comes from God: we can no more confer grace on ourselves than our lungs can manufacture the air we breathe. Yet in the divine–human relationship the individual Christian also has his unique and indispensable contribution to make: the effort to lead a good life, the practice of piety, the performance of deeds of Christlike service to others—all that is customarily embraced in the program of Christian living goes hand in glove with God's redeeming intervention in our lives. We do not save ourselves, but we will not be saved *despite* ourselves or apart from cooperation with Jesus. We must do the good deeds, live the life that God has prepared for us.

It is particularly important to make this point in regard to suffering. Its passive character—something we undergo, not something we do—might seem to indicate that, in this area at least, passivity is all that is required. But that is not so. A very active response is required of us: the effort to cultivate and sustain the disposition of joining our suffering to the suffering of Jesus. (Here too God's grace is needed both to commence and to continue this undertaking; yet our cooperation with grace is required, in this case as in any other, for the divine–human collaboration to succeed.)

Despite all such necessary disclaimers, the fundamental fact is that the unity of Christ with his members, and of the members with one another, is real. It is much more than moral solidarity. It is a true, dynamic unity, best thought of on an organic model. We are incorporated into Christ and his Mystical Body through baptism; by grace we participate in divine life; through the Eucharist we enjoy bodily union with Jesus' Resurrection-life and so with one another. Moreover, something revolutionary follows from all this. Our life is life in and through Christ; all our ordinary, everyday deeds become elements of our living in Christ; in particular, by accepting our suffering and death in union with him, we suffer and die in the Lord.

How is all this related to suffering? Not only is suffering part of human life, the evidence is overwhelming that, in Jesus' plan, it is also meant to play a special role in Christian life. What is that role?

Certain themes stand out among the many answers that have been proposed. One is that suffering strengthens character, fosters conversion, and leads us to recognize and accept our dependence on God. Speaking of the "special grace" that suffering possesses to draw persons "interiorly close to Christ," Pope John Paul writes:

> To this grace many saints, such as Saint Francis of Assisi, Saint Ignatius of Loyola and others, owe their profound conversion. A result of such a conversion is not only that the individual discovers the salvific meaning of suffering but above all that he becomes a completely new

person. He discovers a new dimension, as it were, of his entire life and vocation.... This interior maturity and spiritual greatness in suffering are certainly the result of a particular conversion and cooperation with the grace of the Crucified Redeemer.

In human beings, conversion seems to stand on a border where the psychological and the spiritual meet. Considered from the psychological side, it is the culmination of a process of change to which suffering can contribute. For suffering obliges us to confront a disconcerting but crucial fact about ourselves: we are living in a desperate condition and are desperately in need of the mercy of God.

If it is only a partial explanation of suffering to say, as the Old Testament sometimes does, that suffering is punishment for sin, it is perfectly true that suffering can lead people to seek remedies for their sinfulness. Sin, in our fallen state, supplies a large part of our environment. We take sin and its consequences for granted; we regard evil with complacency, as people raised in a sewer would consider perpetual darkness and stench to be natural and normal. Suffering can shock us out of this potentially disastrous state of mind; from this point of view we can think of it as one way God has of getting our attention, breaking down unfounded self-reliance, and impressing upon us our absolute need for help.

In this context C. S. Lewis identifies three purposes served by pain. The first is to awaken us to the reality of our desperate situation, menaced by sin on all sides—and from within—and certain to succumb unless we turn entirely to God. Suffering can lead to repentance and amendment. The second purpose is to take away our illusory contentment with things as they are and make it clear that lasting satisfaction will be found, if at all, only in God. The third is to purify and focus our intention—to leave us no alternative to acting for love of God (such an alternative, say, as acting for love of self), since it is impossible joyfully to accept pain for any other motive.

Yet Christian apologetics must be careful not to romanticize suffering, making it out to be a foolproof instrument for either psychological or spiritual growth. It is true that pain can strengthen character, but it can also destroy it, reducing the one who suffers to a physical and moral shambles prepared to commit any crime or endure any humiliation in order to obtain relief. It is true that suffering can turn thoughts away from self and worldliness and in the direction of God, thus fostering conversion and a flourishing of the interior life; but it can also sap the capacity for attending to spiritual concerns and, at the extreme, can cause people either to stop believing in God or to regard him with bitterness and horror.

Emphatically, these considerations apply to the most profound meaning of suffering—that it is our participation in the Passion of Jesus Christ and, as such, is co-redemptive. This is true; it flows from everything said up to now about Christian life as dynamic unity with Christ, by which we live in him and he in us. Yet this truth hardly takes away the sting of suffering. Ideally, as Pope John Paul says, a person reflecting on his sufferings in this light "rediscovers them, through faith, enriched with a new content and new meaning." But the process is complex, and the result far from certain.

The understanding of suffering as co-redemptive is stated with exceptional clarity by the sixteenth-century theologian Cajetan.

> A clearer and more persuasive way to explain this merit is to show that it is not so much our work as the work of Christ our Head, acting in us and through us.
>
> For we must suppose, as the Apostle does when he writes to the Romans (12:5), to the Ephesians (4:12–16), and to the Colossians (2:9–11), that men in the state of grace are the living members of Christ. We must also suppose that the union of Christ our Head with those men who are His living members is not like that of a political body . . . but that the Head and members form one body, as in a natural body. Christ the Head vivifies the members by His spirit, and, as St. Paul plainly teaches, He unites them together by means of spiritual joints and bonds.
>
> Again, we must suppose, as the Scripture teaches, that the sufferings and actions of Christ's living members are the sufferings and actions of Christ, their Head. On the subject of their sufferings, we have Christ's own words:

"Saul, Saul, why dost thou persecute Me?" (Acts 9:4) Yet Paul was persecuting only His members. And Paul reminds the Galatians (Gal 3: 1) that Christ was crucified in them, by which he clearly means, in the sufferings they have endured for Christ. On the subject of their actions, St. Paul writes to the Corinthians (2 Cor 13:3): "Seek ye a proof of Christ who speaketh in me?" Finally, speaking in general, he tells the Galatians (2: 20, D.V.): "I live, now not I, but Christ liveth in me."

From all this, I conclude that it is perfectly true for me to say: "I merit; no, it is not I who merit, but Christ who merits in me. I fast; now not I, for it is Christ that fasts within me, and so of all the free actions that the living members of Christ perform for God."

When we suffer, it is Jesus who suffers in us. Not that we become mere passive instruments: Jesus has opened his suffering to our *participation*; when we suffer in and for Christ, we participate in the redemptive action of Jesus. Eugene Boylan says, "We can regard our actions at any moment as performed in partnership with Christ on the cross." And Caryll Houselander exclaims, "We are now beginning in very earnest to experience the contemplation which consists in suffering with Christ, and the way to sanctify it is not so much to suffer with Him as to ask Him to let us realize that it is He who suffers in us."

These are not isolated outbursts; they are expressions of mainstream Christian tradition. "But," someone of a prosaic turn of mind might object, "all this sounds like mysticism!" Perhaps so; and perhaps it is mystics who come closest to expressing the inner reality of Christian life. In any case, someone troubled by the literalism of statements like these would not be mistaken in adopting the view that, as our relationship with Jesus can be understood as an exceptionally intense moral union, so the relationship of our suffering to his can be understood as one of sympathy and conscious, deliberate imitation. The only contrary point I wish to make concerns the extensive and persuasive testimony that the full reality far exceeds that true but limited view.

Pope John Paul writes: "Every man has his own share in the Redemption. Each one is also called to share in that suffering through which the Redemption was accomplished." And again: "Insofar as man becomes a sharer in Christ's sufferings—in any part of the world and at any time in history—to that extent he in his own way completes the suffering through which Christ accomplishes the Redemption of the world."

The notion of "completing" Jesus' suffering by our own recalls an important aspect of Paul's statement in Colossians: "I complete what is lacking in Christ's afflictions" (Col 1:24). Is it possible to speak of Jesus' suffering as "lacking" in some significant sense? Did Jesus in fact fail to accomplish the Redemption, so that Christians individually and together must now take up the uncompleted task and bring it to successful fulfillment?

Evidently not. "Christ achieved the Redemption

completely and to the very limit," the Holy Father writes, "but at the same time he did not bring it to a close. . . . It seems to be part of the very essence of Christ's redemptive suffering that this suffering requires to be unceasingly completed."

There is a very imperfect parallel in other human actions that in a sense require the participation of others for their completeness. As I write I am conscious that, while from one point of view my act of writing is complete as soon as I set the words on paper, from another point of view the totality of the action I envisage requires the dynamic cooperation of another party, the reader, striving to assimilate the ideas and make them his own. And, as the unity between Christ and his members is far more intimate and real than the union between writer and reader, so the relationship between Christ's suffering and ours in the context of redemption is vastly more intimate and interactive than a relationship based on sympathy and imitation alone. "This Redemption," Pope John Paul says,

> even though it was completely achieved by Christ's suffering, lives on and in its own special way develops in the history of man. It lives and develops as the body of Christ, the Church, and in this dimension every human suffering, by reason of the loving union with Christ, completes the suffering of Christ. It completes the suffering just as the Church completes the redemptive work of Christ.

It is important to introduce this communal dimension into the discussion and not focus exclusively on our isolated, individual lives as Christians. Jesus' redemptive work was precisely the setting up of a new covenant, establishing the communion between God and man in its definitive form. Although his suffering, death, and Resurrection were complete and sufficient to establish the new covenant community, nevertheless an element of incompleteness in the work of redemption remains until the community itself participates in what its Founder and Redeemer has done.

We participate in two ways. First, we receive the benefit of membership in this communion, incorporation into Christ, through the moral commitment of faith celebrated in baptism, through the bodily communion of the Eucharist, and through the grace of the Spirit pouring love into our hearts. Second, we make our response by cooperating with Jesus and the Spirit in our own sanctification, as well as by cooperating as a united, covenant community in Jesus' mission, the apostolate. Paul emphasizes this in his letter to the Colossians, where he speaks of suffering with Christ for the sake of the Church. Suffering and the Christian apostolate are intimately linked: suffering for the sake of Christ and the Church is an apostolic activity, while the struggle to carry out the apostolate inevitably brings one into conflict with the forces of evil and causes one to experience suffering.

As members of the Mystical Body, we live with Christ, we suffer with him, and we co-redeem with him. Had there been no Jesus, we would still suffer, but our suffering would be as many people still continue to experience it: sterile and meaningless. As it is, Jesus has transformed our lives and, specifically, our suffering by giving us a role with him in the work of redemption. "Man's sorrows continue to be Christ's sorrows, Christ's passion," Caryll Houselander writes. "They continue to atone for sin. All the suffering we see today, all the suffering we know in our own lives, is the Passion of Christ."

It is not, of course, as if we literally reenact our Lord's Passion in all its concrete specificity. Jesus instructs his followers to identify themselves with him unconditionally and to follow him without reserve, even to the point of assuming the cross: "He who does not take his cross and follow me is not worthy of me" (Mt 10:38). But it is *our own crosses*—the particular tribulations and sufferings of *our* lives—that we are to bear in practicing discipleship. It would be a perversion of Christian spirituality to dwell in imagination upon the suffering of Jesus, supposing that one was thereby participating in his Passion, while at the same time rejecting or rebelling against the grubby, concrete, disagreeable trials that come one's way in the course of one's own life. The way of co-redemption is precisely the way of coming face to face with one's own misery and accepting it for the same reason that Jesus accepted his suffering. In this way, even the trivial wretchedness of our everyday lives—fatigue, pain, disappointment of all kinds—has redemptive value.

It is true that our lives in their totality—including our joys—are, or can be, co-redemptive. This value, or property, resides in love, fidelity, and responsiveness to God's will, not in suffering as such. Suffering, however, is plainly part of the human condition, part of our lives, and it is to be received and lifted up to the Father like any other element of our experience. Moreover, it is fair to say that, as suffering played a critical role in the redemptive work of Jesus, so it has a special part in our co-redemptive activity.

"Every man has his own share in the Redemption," the Holy Father writes. "Each one is also called to share in that suffering through which the Redemption was accomplished." Pope John Paul goes on to tell us:

> It is this which justifies calling suffering a vocation. Christ does not explain in the abstract the reasons for suffering, but before all else he says: "Follow me!" Come! Take part through your suffering in this work of saving the world, a salvation achieved through my suffering! through my cross. Gradually, as the individual takes up his cross, spiritually uniting himself to the cross of Christ, the salvific meaning of suffering is revealed before him. . . . It is then that man finds in his suffering interior peace and even spiritual joy.

Indeed, as we have seen, because of its co-redemptive character, suffering can properly be seen as a form of apostolate, a sharing in the Church's mission of continuing the redemptive work of Jesus.

"This is a most fruitful field of apostolate for the laity," Eugene Boylan remarks. "Even in the ordinary day's round, they can exercise the apostolate, and, like the heart in the human body, they can associate themselves in the work of 'circulating' the life of Christ in the souls of His members, by prayer and suffering."

The thought is not new. From the earliest times, the suffering associated with persecution has been linked to Christianity in a special way, viewed as a kind of hallmark of the Christian and of Christian life. "For to this you have been called, because Christ also suffered for you, leaving you an example, that you should follow in his steps" (1 Pet 2:21). There is a kind of inevitability here: those who set out resolutely to follow Jesus Christ are bound, it seems, to come into conflict sooner or later with the forces of evil in the world; if they respond as Jesus did—seeking to overcome evil by suffering it with confidence in God, rather than fighting it with evil of their own—they are bound also to experience persecution in some form.

Citing Dietrich Bonhoeffer's observation that "following the way of the cross is sharing Christ's Passion in the world," Jürgen Moltmann points out that in the context of Christian discipleship "cross" does not refer merely to "the discomforts of natural existence" but to "the outward and inward sufferings which arise from the following of the Son of Man in an inhuman world." The Christian should be neither dismayed nor downhearted when this phenomenon appears in his own life or in the life of the Christian community. "Beloved, do not be surprised at the fiery ordeal which comes upon you to prove you, as though something strange were happening to you. But rejoice in so far as you share Christ's sufferings" (1 Pet 4:12–13).

The supreme expression of this is martyrdom. At first glance, the ardor with which countless Christians over the centuries have approached the sacrifice of their lives seems virtually incomprehensible. But against the background we have been examining, the words of St. Ignatius of Antioch, writing to his fellow Christians as he was being carried by soldiers through Asia Minor to be thrown to wild beasts in Rome, make perfectly good sense:

> Suffer me to be the food of the beasts, for through them I can possess God. I am the wheat of God, and I am ground by the teeth of the beasts, that I may be found the pure bread of Jesus Christ. . . . I seek Him who died for us; I desire Him who rose for us; the pains of birth are upon me. Suffer me, my brothers, do not keep me from life. . . . Let me imitate the sufferings of my God. If anyone has Christ within him, let him consider what I wish, and let him sympathize with me.

The suffering and death of martyrdom are the surest way to a new and immeasurably better life than one can possibly know in this world.

Even so, we come up at this point against an immensely difficult problem. It is possible that what has been said up to now makes sense in the case of self-conscious, devout Christians—people who understand their lives, and especially their suffering, as a loving participation in the life and suffering of Jesus Christ and welcome whatever befalls them, no matter how bitter, as a privileged opportunity to share in Jesus' redemptive act, thus benefiting their neighbors while growing in friendship with God. Such persons find meaning and truth in an affirmation like that of St. John of the Cross: "Suffering is a surer and even more advantageous road than that of joy and action."

All this is possible to comprehend and may even be possible, though difficult, to put into practice for people who are mature and highly motivated Christians. But what of people who are not? What good role can suffering play in the lives of those who in no way can be expected to glimpse, much less agree with, the rationale set out here? Does God play favorites, opening the eyes of a few to the divine potential of their suffering while leaving the many to suffer blindly in this life as a prelude to eternal suffering in the next?

Arthur Koestler, in his novel *Darkness at Noon*, refers to "the difference between suffering which makes sense and senseless suffering." That is what is at issue here, and the problem occurs again and again in literature and in life. In *The Brothers Karamazov*, Dostoyevsky depicts Ivan Karamazov grappling with the suffering of innocent children and losing faith in "dear, kind God" because of it; not that Ivan stops believing in God—he merely stops trying to come to terms with a world in which God permits such outrages: "It's not God that I don't accept. . . . Only I must respectfully return Him the ticket."

Charles Journet, speaking of the suffering and death of young children, remarks that the best answer that unaided philosophy is capable of giving to the problem is that "as a whole it is better that pain and death should exist than to want to do away with them and thereby do away with life and sensibility." As for theology, it carries the discussion a bit further, observing that "some sufferings must remain without consolation in this life, that Christ sheds light on them without consoling them, and that their consolation will come only in Heaven." Both statements are true, but neither is very satisfying.

The question being asked here is, in fact, one to which we have been given no clear and definitive answer and which, in the nature of things, we can scarcely begin to answer for ourselves in humanly satisfying terms. Faith sheds light on the matter, but its light is flickering and obscure. And yet in this light we do see at least the outlines of an explanation—the explanation to which Caryll Houselander refers in speaking of " 'unconscious Christs'; people who . . . share His life and Passion without knowing it."

Jacques Maritain writes of people such as these in an essay called "Blessed Are the Persecuted." Recalling the suffering of millions of innocents during

World War II, he points to the evident fact that they "did not give their lives, their lives were taken from them.... They suffered without having wanted to suffer" or knowing why they suffered. Nor were they alone in this. Time and again this phenomenon of unsought, uncomprehended suffering repeats itself. Where in the Christian understanding of suffering is there room for this?

"It all seems to take place," Maritain writes, "as though the death agony of Jesus—being so divinely vast—must be divided into its contrasting aspects in order that some image of it might pass into His members, and that men might completely participate in this great treasure of love." This seems to point in the direction of two quite different experiences of suffering. "The saints"—or, perhaps it would be better to say, conscious Christians deliberately trying to realize the implications that unity with Christ has for their suffering—"of their own will enter into Christ's passion, offering themselves along with Him, in knowing the secrets of the divine life, in living in their souls their union with Him." These are the "privileged people" for whom the experience of suffering is illuminated by the radically new redemptive meaning given to it by the Passion of Jesus Christ.

But what of those who suffer without seeking or understanding, those who, as Maritain says, are "hurled into Christ's death agony without knowing it and without wanting it"? They are making manifest another aspect of the same agony, the aspect expressed in Jesus' cry of abandonment from the cross, "My God, my God, why hast thou forsaken me?" (Mk 15: 34). And Maritain concludes:

> The great flock of the truly destitute, of those dead without consolation—would He not take care of those who bear this mark of His agony? How could it happen that their very forsaking itself would not serve as the signature of their belonging to the crucified Savior, and as a supreme title to His mercy?
>
> For them there are not signs, for them hope is stripped as bare as they are themselves; for them, to the bitter end, nothing, even from the direction of God, has shone forth in men's eyes. It is in the invisible world, beyond everything earthly, that the kingdom of God is given to these persecuted ones, and that everything becomes theirs.

To a great extent, this is true for us all. No matter how enlightened by faith our understanding of suffering may be, or how moved by charity our acceptance of it, it is in hope—hope that looks beyond the experience—that we find reason and strength to bear it. "I consider that the sufferings of this present time are not worth comparing with the glory that is to be revealed to us" (Rom 8: 18). Finally, it is the hope of resurrection that makes it possible for us to sustain the agony of death.

The Resurrection of Jesus Christ is the incontrovertible sign of redemption. It is the Father's eloquent testimony that Jesus' perfect fidelity, ultimately expressed in his wretched death on the cross, has truly overcome evil and opened the way of salvation to his followers. It is the conclusive demonstration that Jesus' suffering and death accomplished what they were meant to accomplish.

And so with us: our hope of resurrection contains an implicit affirmation that by fidelity to God's will in the face of suffering we participate in the redemption won for us by Christ. As Pope John Paul remarks, cross and Resurrection are inseparably linked in the life of Christ and in the lives of Christians: "Those who share in the sufferings of Christ are also called, through their own sufferings, to share in glory." Resurrection is the outcome of redemption; suffering is the path that leads us there.

IV

Suffering in Christian Life

What, then, are we to make of suffering—is it helpful or is it not? St. Teresa of Avila says, "It is to those whom my Father loves most dearly that he sends the greatest trials; for love and trials go together." William Styron points out in one of his novels that "despite the dreck that's been written in the Gospels, adversity produces not understanding and compassion, but cruelty." Who is right?

Most people, I suspect, would like to agree with St. Teresa. It is consoling to think of suffering as a mark of God's favor. If it does not make suffering easy to bear, at least it makes it more nearly tolerable. Unfortunately, though, the statement that adversity produces cruelty is all too often verified in our experience. Some of us may be ennobled by suffering, but others are debased.

It has been said that mystics are people who have learned to regard suffering as a means of purification and as a vocation. Most of us are not mystics, but it may be that we are meant to develop whatever "mystical" talents we possess in order to make sense of suffering. Coming face to face with extreme suffering with only everyday resources at one's disposal—a commonsense, reasonable way of thinking, a disposition generally to put up with what life sends one's way (provided it doesn't cross the border between the bearable and the unbearable), a sense of humor that fails only when things that really matter are imperiled, nerves no more or less steady than the next person's—one is very likely to fail the test. Something more is needed.

Before the fact, none of us should take it for granted that we will respond well to great suffering. We can be certain only that suffering, when it comes, will test us to our limits and disclose whether our prior view of suffering, whatever it might have been, was an authentic expression of character or a sham.

In 1940 C. S. Lewis published a small book called *The Problem of Pain.* I have been much in its debt in writing this book, and I recommend it highly. Lewis was an honest and tough-minded Christian apologist. Yet *The Problem of Pain* does present difficulties. It is a little too pat. There is an answer for every question. The answers are intelligent, often brilliant; they may even be correct. The difficulty is that any attempt to "explain" suffering that ignores, or seems to ignore, its mysteriousness is ultimately unsatisfying and can be scandalous.

Lewis returned to this theme many years after he wrote *The Problem of Pain.* His second book on this topic is *A Grief Observed.* It is a spiritual journal, composed in the weeks immediately after his wife's death. In it, faith itself comes close to buckling under the strain. "Not that I am (I think) in much danger of ceasing to believe in God," Lewis writes, "the real danger is of coming to believe such dreadful things about him."

In time Lewis's faith won out over his suffering—or, more precisely perhaps, his suffering was integrated into the context of faith. My purpose, however, is not to cite him as a model or exemplar but to make a simpler point: it is possible to "understand" suffering with great clarity, even to the point of being able to "explain" it to oneself and others; yet such understanding and explanatory power are of an entirely different order from, and no substitute at all for, the strength to accept and "use" suffering, which comes only from living faith.

How, then, can we cultivate living faith with this end in view?

We can begin by putting aside one false notion—that the appropriate Christian response to suffering is tight-lipped stoicism and indifference to pain. Dom Columba Marmion makes a useful distinction between "complaining" and "murmuring." The latter "implies opposition, malevolence"—it is resistance to the will of God. But complaining is "in nowise an imperfection, it may even be a prayer. . . . It is the cry of a heart that is crushed, that feels suffering, but accepts it entirely, and lovingly." The model for this Christian "complaining" is Christ on the cross.

As we have seen repeatedly, however, Christ is more than just our "model" in this or any other aspect of Christian life. Certainly we ought consciously to pattern our behavior on his, to search out his thoughts and form our minds by them, to learn his will and conform ours to his; reflective, prayerful reading of the Gospels is one excellent way of doing this. But beyond such conscious imitation of Jesus lies the relationship of mystical unity about which spiritual writers, beginning with St. Paul, speak with such force and eloquence. Unity with Jesus commences in baptism, the sacrament of our dying and rising with the Lord, the initiation of an authentic "new life"—life in Jesus Christ. But baptism is only the beginning. This new life is meant to continue, grow, and intensify. Preeminently this comes about through the Eucharist.

"He will come to you every day in the Holy Sacrament," Marmion writes, "in order to change you into Himself." That is exactly the point. There is nothing wrong with explanations of the Blessed Sacrament that speak of it as nourishing and strengthening the interior life: so it does. The relevant question, though, is *how* it does this.

The answer is that the Blessed Sacrament works, so to speak, by uniting us to Jesus (as well as to one another in the Mystical Body) and in this way, in a certain sense, changing us into himself. Vatican Council II, quoting St. Leo the Great, makes this point: "The partaking of the Body and Blood of Christ does nothing other than transform us into that which we consume." But the insight can be traced even further back—to Jesus himself, espe-

cially in the eucharistic discourse in the sixth chapter
of John's Gospel and in the Last Supper discourse:

> I am the true vine, and my Father is the vine-
> dresser. Every branch of mine that bears no
> fruit, he takes away, and every branch that does
> bear fruit he prunes, that it may bear more
> fruit. . . . I am the vine, you are the branches. He
> who abides in me, and I in him, he it is that
> bears much fruit, for apart from me you can do
> nothing (Jn 15: 1–2, 5).

Already these words contain a compact doctrine
of suffering: "Every branch that does bear fruit he
prunes." Suffering is a purgative experience, ori-
ented to a positive outcome: spiritual fruitfulness.
Another name for this is co-redemption. Because of
our unity with Christ, the gifts we offer the Father
are acceptable and efficacious: we do have roles to
play in God's redemptive plan.

The Eucharist, then, is the preeminent means for
deepening and intensifying our unity with Jesus
and thus conferring redemptive meaning on our
lives, including, especially, our suffering. There are,
however, other valuable ways of learning and intensifying the Christian meaning of suffering. One is
self-denial.

Self-denial does not have a good reputation these
days. It is associated in people's minds with the
gloomy side of religion, complete with hair shirts,
disciplines, and long faces. That innumerable saints
over the centuries have practiced detachment,

asceticism, mortification, and resignation and com-
mended them to others is taken to be a merely
historical circumstance illustrating that saints can
be wrong. Perhaps they also believed that the earth
is flat; we need no more be guided by their views on
penance than by their views on the shape of the
planet.

There is a certain truth in this critique. Some
practices of the past *do* seem excessive by contemporary standards. Strenuous fasts, disabling
physical penances—perhaps these things were of
spiritual advantage to those who practiced them in
times gone by, but that is no reason to urge them on
people today. For the vast majority of Christians,
living in the world, the appropriate ascetical regi-
men is one that, among other things, enables them
to respond vigorously to the demands of their secular environment; excessive penances do not meet
that prescription.

Granted. But does it follow that there is no place
in Christian life for *any* self-denial? Evidently not.

The tradition's testimony is simply too strong:
self-denial is an essential element in Christian life;
there can hardly be a spirituality worthy of the
name without it.

Dom Columba Marmion writes: "The more our
souls, by means of mortification, free themselves
from sin and are detached from self and creatures,
the more the divine action is powerful within us."
C. S. Lewis writes: "Hence the necessity to die daily:
however often we think we have broken the rebel-

lious self we shall still find it alive." Josemaría Escrivá de Balaguer writes: "Where there is no mortification, there is no virtue." These are not voices out of the Dark Ages; they speak to us here and now.

The difficulty with self-denial seems to arise from two sources: confusion over what it is and confusion over the purpose or purposes it is meant to serve.

Let us start with the question of purpose. There are several. First, asceticism properly so-called is a kind of training, not unlike the training of athletes. It is a systematic approach to overcoming, or at least reducing, the tugs toward self-indulgence and immediate gratification we all experience. Not that pleasure is intrinsically wrong and to be avoided at all times. In fact, though, we know that pleasure often does serve as a kind of bait, drawing us toward behavior that is wrong.

The purpose of asceticism is to train us in the art of deferring or forgoing gratifications, so that, when a real test comes, we will not drop our defenses at the first glimpse of a tempting pleasure and blunder into immorality in pursuit of it. Through asceticism we learn to some extent to anticipate and resist those blind, instinctive lunges that, unanticipated and unresisted, so easily end in evil. When, furthermore, the aim is to root out sin in our lives, the practice is what is properly called mortification. This "putting to death" is nothing other than a systematic campaign against mortal and venial sin.

It is in this sense that asceticism becomes, as Étienne Gilson points out, an expression of Christian optimism:

> The world that the Christian detests consists of all that mass of disorder, deformity and evil introduced into creation by man's own voluntary defection. He turns away from these, no doubt, but precisely to adhere with all his heart to the order, beauty and good which was willed from the beginning. . . . Nothing could be more positive than such an asceticism, nothing could be better grounded in hope and resolute optimism.

Yet another purpose of self-denial is expressed by St. Paul: "I have been crucified with Christ; it is no longer I who live, but Christ who lives in me"; "those who belong to Christ Jesus have crucified the flesh with its passions and desires" (Gal 2: 20; 5: 24). By self-denial we become less, so that Christ may be more in us. "It is," says Eugene Boylan, "the getting rid of self in order to allow Jesus to live His life in us . . . an 'assertion' of Jesus rather than a denial of self." And, useful as external practices may be, it is clear from this perspective that internal mortifications, directed to acquiring and practicing the indispensable virtue of humility, are of primary importance.

Ultimately, of course, there is the co-redemptive value of self-denial, considered as a special instance of suffering. The passage from Colossians that forms the basis for this entire discussion suggests how we are to participate with Christ in his work of expiation; the application of the merits of Jesus' Passion to individuals seems, in a sense, to depend on our prayers and sufferings. Boylan observes that Christians, "like the heart in the human body . . . can associate themselves in the work of 'circulating' the life of Christ in the souls of His members, by prayer and suffering." Self-denial in the form of resignation—acceptance, out of love of God, of the evil that befalls us—is one way to do this.

There are differing views on whether it is a good idea to seek out penances and inflict them on oneself. Perhaps the background of this disagreement is the memory of the seemingly excessive self-inflicted mortifications of some Christians in times gone by; whatever might be said for such practices by particular individuals in their particular circumstances, they are not to be recommended generally, nor do they seem to have much relevance to Christian life in the world today. But this does not rule out *all* self-imposed acts of self-denial; on the contrary, it leaves very broad latitude for small, unobtrusive measures of self-conquest, both those practiced on a regular, planned basis and those carried out spontaneously.

At the same time, it is probably even more important that, instead of going out of our way to seek and practice penance, we approach everyday life in a spirit of readiness to take advantage of the opportunities for self-denial through detachment and resignation that naturally arise: getting up on time when we don't feel like it; being agreeable to others even *before* the first cup of coffee; practicing courtesy and consideration for others (especially those who are rude) on the way to work and in the workplace, the classroom, the supermarket; deferring to family members in little things ("What do *you* want to watch on TV?"); and so on.

Writing of London air raids during World War II, Caryll Houselander offers this account of "routine" mortification:

> A raid gives the opportunity of countless little acts of love, such as making a cup of tea, lending a pillow or a rug, giving up the best place, controlling our own feelings in order to help others to be calm and plucky, and, when it can be done without irritating, reminding people that they are in the hands of God; or contriving to make them laugh.

Most of us are unlikely to be called on to practice mortification in such dramatic circumstances, but we all have many opportunities to observe Escrivá's prescription for a sound program of dying to self:

> The appropriate word you left unsaid; the joke you didn't tell; the cheerful smile for those who bother you; that silence when you're unjustly accused; your kind conversation with people you find boring and tactless; the daily effort to overlook one irritating detail or another in those who live with you . . . this, with perseverance, is indeed solid interior mortification.

What, finally, ought our attitude toward suffering be? There are several possibilities.

A secularist views suffering as ultimate, absolute evil. This view expresses itself in two vastly different forms of external behavior—hedonism and social activism. The hedonist's fundamental commitment is to avoiding suffering through the pursuit of pleasure. Gratification, coarse in some cases but refined in others, is an antidote to pain. This is a case of that alienation typical of secularized Western society, which in its simplest form expresses itself as systematic escapism.

It is quite otherwise with the secular social activist, whose energies are devoted above all to removing suffering. This commitment has led to many deeds that have helped make life more bearable for countless persons. One thinks of the work of dedicated doctors and nurses, scientific researchers, the authors and implementers of innumerable private and governmental programs for the alleviation of poverty and the eradication of its causes. Their efforts deserve admiration and imitation.

But there is a problem. The secular reformer's fundamental commitment is to the removal of suffering. All else failing, this can lead to proposals for removing those who suffer: hence such things as the killing of handicapped infants before or after birth, euthanasia, and various murderous projects executed on a massive scale throughout this century in the name of eugenics or social revolution.

Plainly, many secular reformers abhor such deeds and would under no circumstances be guilty of taking life. But the *ideology* of secularistic reform is another matter. Whether it takes its inspiration from socialist or liberal-democratic sources, it views suffering as the ultimate enemy, and its natural inclination is to do whatever is required, up to and including the taking of life—all in order to put an end to suffering.

This critique needs a cautionary note, however. Religious persons sometimes devote so much energy to berating secularists that they seem to have little left for the good works that occupy secular humanitarians. This is not acceptable: the Christian must work as hard as the secularist to alleviate suffering and remove its causes; the difference, as Houselander says, is that "where he [the Christian] fails to heal it he must share it." And more:

> We have something which even our own unworthiness cannot take away from us, which belongs to even those of us who are the greatest human failures, and which can be given to others only through us. This is the doctrine of suffering, the revelation of God about suffering. It is in this doctrine that hope and meaning and comfort exist, and this is ours.

But we do not necessarily come to this point quickly or easily. The pain of suffering is as great for Christians as it is for others, and it can obscure, temporarily or even permanently, the "doctrine of suffering." Citing Maritain, Charles Journet speaks of a Christian dialectic of suffering marked by three distinct stages.

In the first stage, suffering is viewed simply as

natural to the human condition and is accepted with pained resignation. But because this is *Christian* suffering, there is the further recognition that the situation must be borne patiently for love of God. This is no little thing. It is far from clear that all Christians reach even this first stage.

The second is a reaction to the first. The naturalness and inevitability of suffering are questioned. Original Sin is considered not to account for all suffering. Thus the suffering of the innocent, of those guilty of no *personal* offense, is regarded as scandalous and absurd. Journet calls this "the stage of outraged Christian suffering." Lately we have seen it in the advocates of some forms of liberation theology, whose indignation at the oppression of the poor led them to adopt Marxist notions—class struggle and revolutionary violence—as the solution to the evil they found in society.

The Christian at the third stage of the dialectic sees the suffering of the innocent as a consequence of Original Sin, but he does not on that account regard suffering as merely inevitable, to be passively endured. Rather, understanding it as a participation in the suffering of Christ, he considers it co-redemptive. Says Journet:

> Christ did not choose suffering because it was good. Suffering was an evil for him insofar as he was a person. But he willed to undergo it so as to save the world. And in this way, as Christ's chosen instrument in his redemptive work, suffering has become good. And therefore, insofar as

they believe their suffering to be a sharing in Christ's sufferings, the saints love and cherish it as a treasure *because of him,* as the suffering of Christ shared by them.

But, he hastens to add, "not in any way just as suffering, for as such it is always hateful." In Gethsemane Jesus prayed to the Father, "Remove this cup from me." For him, as for us, suffering was repugnant; could he have done so and still carried out his commitment to remain faithful to the Father's will, he would have shunned it. Yet the rest of his prayer is no less significant: "Yet not what I will, but what thou wilt" (Mk 14:36). Sanctity consists, finally, in uniting oneself with God's will. This is eminently true of the sanctity that comes through suffering.

Therefore, at every stage of the Christian dialectic, even (for those who reach it) the highest, simple patience in the face of suffering remains indispensable. "The virtue that I want to find in you on our next meeting," writes Columba Marmion, "is above all *patience.*" He goes on to explain:

> This life is not given by God as a Paradise. It is a time of trial followed by an eternity of joy and rest. Christ suffered all His life, for the shadow of the cross ever hung over Him, and those who love Him share His cross to some extent all their life long. The contrarieties, the misunderstandings, the sufferings of heart and body, household difficulties, all these things form the portion of your cross, and when you accept these trials they become holy and divine by their union with those of Jesus Christ.

Nor should this be an expression of mere stoic endurance. Escrivá de Balaguer speaks of a smiling asceticism as part of the Christian ideal. This is not hard to understand. The Christian life is a life of joy, and it is possible, through love, to retain a spirit of joyfulness even alongside suffering.

Possible—but not easy. One difficulty repeatedly encountered by those who aspire to suffer in this spirit is the absence of consolation, the seeming lack of support and encouragement from God at the time of trial. "When you are happy," C. S. Lewis remarks, "you will be—or so it feels—welcomed with open arms. But go to Him when your need is desperate, when all other help is vain, and what do you find? A door slammed in your face, and a sound of bolting and double bolting on the inside."

How explain this? In part, on the basis that our experience of God's absence in suffering mirrors that of Jesus: "My God, my God, why hast thou forsaken me?" (Mt 27:46). True, these words come from a messianic psalm that, beginning with the Redeemer's experience of dereliction, concludes by affirming confidence in God's salvific power: "He has not despised or abhorred the affliction of the afflicted; and he has not hid his face from him, but has heard, when he cried to him" (Ps 22:24). Yet neither in the psalm nor in the Passion of Christ nor in our own suffering is the experience of desolation any less real because it coexists with faith and hope in God's loving constancy. At the nadir of his suffering, Jesus *felt* himself abandoned by the Father; so do we at the nadir of ours.

What we really experience, though, is not so much God's absence as the lack of consolation. The distinction is important. It may be that, if we felt too consoled, we would rest content in the experience of consolation, rather than reaching out in distress and desolation to the Father who seems absent. Consolation is good, but it is not God; perhaps one must lack it so as not to make the mistake of settling for a lesser good. Otherwise, one might deserve the rebuke of Josemaría Escrivá de Balaguer: "Come, now! After saying so often, 'The cross, Lord, the cross,' it is obvious you wanted a cross to your own taste."

Approaching the end of this book, I am aware that I have said relatively little, directly and explicitly at least, about what Pope John Paul II in *Salvifici doloris* speaks of as the second Christian meaning of suffering: namely, the suffering of others and the opportunity it affords—as well as the obligation it imposes—for us to respond. Much has been written on this subject in recent years. What is less clear and often, indeed, a matter of controversy is the concrete form that the Christian response to the suffering of others ought to take, especially when this response is envisaged as having a political dimension. It is an important debate but beyond the scope of this book. Those interested in pursuing the matter will find important insights in the *Instruction on Christian Freedom and Liberation*, published in 1986 by the Congregation for the Doctrine of the Faith, as well as in its *Instruction on Certain Aspects of the Theology of Liberation* (1984).

At the same time, we need to pause with the Holy Father and reflect on this meaning in the context of the parable of the Good Samaritan. "It indicates," he says,

> what the relationship of each of us must be toward our suffering neighbor. We are not allowed to "pass by on the other side" indifferently; we must "stop" beside him. Everyone who stops beside the suffering of another person, whatever form it may take, is a Good Samaritan. This stopping does not mean curiosity but availability.

It also means, I think, not just pausing but staying, even, or especially, when our staying does not seem to be doing much good. Most of us are driven by results, and this is true of how we relate to suffering quite as much as anything else. In return for our investment (time, compassion, money, whatever), we want to see something happen—*we want the situation to improve*. We are quick to lose patience with suffering that persists despite our best efforts to remove it; from this, it is an easy step to shrugging one's shoulders and walking away.

In doing so, one may even blame the person or persons one has been trying to help: "He's incorrigible." "She doesn't really want to change." "They don't appreciate what you do for them." These judgments may, in fact, be correct; in some cases they may dictate radical changes in the tactics of helping (less doing for the other, more insistence that he do for himself). But that they justify abandoning another to his suffering is very much to be doubted. All we may finally be able to do for some who suffer is to remain with them. If so, that is precisely the service we are called to render, for as long as need be and in the face of our ordinary expectation that things will—*must*—change for the better. It was the service rendered by Mary at the foot of the cross.

This idea of service underlines another aspect of the parable to which Pope John Paul attaches great importance: *everyone* has an obligation to respond individually to the suffering around him. The Pope highly commends the "Good Samaritan work" of religious and secular institutions; but he adds that the institutionalization of the response to suffering is not sufficient. "The institutions are very important and indispensable; nevertheless, no institution by itself can replace the human heart, human compassion, human love or human initiative, when it is a question of dealing with the sufferings of another."

Some reasons for responding to the needs of those who suffer are so obvious they hardly need stating; or, if there is anyone to whom they are not obvious, merely stating them is unlikely to do much good. Simple humanitarian motives impel us in this direction, but so do considerations of a specifically

Christian nature. Perhaps the most compelling of these is that Jesus Christ is himself present in the suffering.

> When the Son of Man comes in his glory, and all the angels with him, then he will sit on his glorious throne. Before him will be gathered all the nations, and he will separate them one from another as a shepherd separates the sheep from the goats, and he will place the sheep at his right hand, but the goats at the left. Then the King will say to those at his right hand: "Come, O blessed of my Father, inherit the kingdom prepared for you from the foundation of the world! For I was hungry and you gave me food, I was thirsty and you gave me drink, I was a stranger and you welcomed me, I was naked and you clothed me, I was sick and you visited me, I was in prison and you came to me." Then the righteous will answer him, "Lord, when did we see thee hungry and feed thee, or thirsty and give thee drink? And when did we see thee a stranger and welcome thee, or naked and clothe thee? And when did we see thee sick or in prison and visit thee?" And the King will answer them, "Truly, I say to you, as you did it to one of the least of these my brethren, you did it to me" (Mt 25:31–40).

And the condemned? "Truly, I say to you, as you did it not to one of the least of these, you did it not to me" (Mt 25:45). Mersch adds, "His final and glorious coming will render testimony to another coming, which is secret and perpetual. . . . His coming before the world will simply attest the fact that all this time He has been present in men's souls and in the Church."

Service to those who suffer will usually include efforts to alleviate their suffering, but, especially where no significant alleviation is possible, it should always include offering support and encouragement. This is the essence of compassion, "suffering with" another. And here a special aspect of compassion needs mention: helping those who suffer to suffer well.

Of course the subject must be approached with a certain caution. Helping others "suffer well" can degenerate into the complacent, insensitive preaching of "resignation" for which Christians have sometimes been criticized. There is even the danger that this approach to suffering may lend support to those who inflict it. Christians are not meant to act as the agents of oppressors, by urging their victims to be passive and "resigned" in the face of misery.

But there remains a true and important sense in which it is part of our task to help others suffer well, just as it is part of our task to suffer well ourselves. What is in question here is suffering that cannot be avoided, suffering that must be undergone in any case. The Christian obligation in these circumstances is to help others understand and use their suffering according to the mind of Christ.

Caryll Houselander says of the secular humanitarian that "where he cannot heal, he can pass by, where he cannot end poverty, he can forsake it." The Christian may do the same, but he at least knows he is shirking an obligation. "He, like the other, has the duty of sharing in the world's effort to break down human misery, but where he fails to heal it he must share it; he can never, with a clean heart, pass it by." And more than that: "The Christian knows that if sorrow comes to an end, the world would come to an end with it. While this world lasts, poverty and pain and death will last too, the torment of the sensitive will go on. And while these things go on, that response of the Christian must go on."

It is necessary to suffer well. When done in co-redemptive union with the Passion of Jesus Christ, suffering deserves to be called, as Pope John Paul and others have called it, a vocation. "Christ does not explain in the abstract the reasons for suffering, but before all else he says: 'Follow me!' Come! Take part through your suffering in this work of saving the world, a salvation achieved through my suffering! Through my cross."

Not that suffering itself is ever anything but the experience of evil. Yet it can be the occasion and the instrument of moral good and so, paradoxically, a cure for evil. "The paradox," Maritain says, "lies in the fact that a (physical) evil can act as a remedy for a greater (moral) evil."

In itself, suffering is a passive experience, something one undergoes. Undertaken in the spirit of Christ, however, it becomes a high form of Christian activity, a perfect expression of abandonment to the will of God. Morally speaking, this is among

the most finely honed and difficult of human acts—
a fully deliberate and free act of the will, almost
always in the face of contrary inclinations and need-
ing constantly to be renewed against inducements
to fall away, which nevertheless issues in a seeming
passivity, a letting go to God and what he wants.

In speaking of suffering in this way, are we de-
scribing a Christian duty or merely a lofty ideal that
few are expected to realize? No one is obliged to do
more than he is capable of doing. Simple resignation and patience—or even the desire to be resigned and patient—will very likely be for most of
us the nearest approximation to Jesus' attitude toward suffering that we can manage. And it will be
pleasing to God.

But even so, the highest significance of suffering—co-redemption—is not merely an option for
the Christian. "To follow Jesus," Germain Grisez
writes, "is to make one's own his commitment to
redeem. . . . A commitment to Jesus is a commitment to help him do what he does: to communicate
divine love by apostolic activity." In large measure
this is Christian life; and this view of Christian life as
co-redemptive in its totality is as relevant to our
suffering as to anything else we do.

Finally, the meaning of suffering does not reside
in the experience itself, any more than the meaning
of life is bound up wholly with this world. There is
no "solution" to the problem of pain that does not
take into account the recompense we have been
promised in Heaven.

In the view of secularists, this is the ultimate Christian escapism: to say that all that's wrong with the world—the injustices that cannot be corrected, the debts that cannot be paid, the hurts that cannot be healed—will be righted in Heaven. "Pie in the sky when you die." But the taunt does not settle the question: are the secularists right or are we?

As Christians see it, Heaven is anything but a *deus ex machina*. There is significant continuity between this world and the next, between what we make of ourselves in this life and what we shall be in the life to come; to a great extent, moreover, we shape our eternal destinies by the efforts we make here and now to overcome evil—an "overcoming" that properly lies in redemptive self-giving for love of God and neighbor. In this context, suffering is scarcely without meaning. It is permitted by God, so that in dealing with it co-redemptively we can prepare the persons and the communion in which Heaven consists.

Our model, guide, and main support in this is Jesus. "Undergoing death itself for all of us sinners," the Second Vatican Council says in its *Pastoral Constitution on the Church in the Modern World*, "he taught us by example that we too must shoulder that cross which the world and the flesh inflict upon those who search after peace and justice"; and now

> He summons others to dedicate themselves to the earthly service of men and to make ready the material of the celestial realm by this minis-

try of theirs. . . . For after we have obeyed the
Lord, and in his Spirit nurtured on earth the
values of human dignity, brotherhood and freedom, and indeed all the good fruits of our nature and enterprise, we will find them again, but
freed of stain, burnished and transfigured. This
will be so when Christ hands over to the Father a
kingdom eternal and universal.

Then those who have suffered well in this life—
suffered co-redemptively in the work of overcoming
evil by love—will enjoy the fruits of the promise
proclaimed in Revelation:

> Then I saw a new heaven and a new earth; for
> the first heaven and the first earth had passed
> away, and the sea was no more. And I saw the
> holy city, new Jerusalem, coming down out of
> heaven from God, prepared as a bride adorned
> for her husband; and I heard a great voice from
> the throne saying, "Behold, the dwelling of God
> is with men. He will dwell with them, and they
> shall be his people, and God himself will be with
> them; he will wipe away every tear from their
> eyes, and death shall be no more, neither shall
> there be mourning nor crying nor pain any
> more, for the former things have passed away"
> (Rev 21:1–4).

Acknowledgments

A number of people have been helpful to me in the writing of this book. Those to whom I am particularly indebted are Richard Doerflinger, Germain Grisez, and Rev. Malcolm Kennedy.

Many books and articles have also contributed to the project. Obviously this is particularly true of Pope John Paul II's *Salvifici doloris* (On the Christian Meaning of Human Suffering), an apostolic letter dated February 11, 1984. Other works that I have found helpful and recommend to the reader (though, unfortunately, not all are now in print) include Karl Adam, *The Son of God* (Image Books, 1960); M. Eugene Boylan, *This Tremendous Lover* (Christian Classics, 1996); Josemaría Escrivá de Balaguer, *Christ Is Passing By* (Scepter, 1977), *Friends of God* (Scepter, 1981), *The Way* (Scepter, 1979), and *The Way of the Cross* (Scepter, 1983); Aelred Graham, *The Love of God* (Image Books, 1959); Germain Grisez, *Beyond the New Theism: A Philosophy of Religion* (Univ. of Notre Dame Press, 1975) and *The Way of the Lord Jesus*, volume 1, *Christian Moral Principles* (Franciscan Herald Press, 1984); Caryll Houselander, *This War Is the Passion* (Sheed & Ward,

1941); Charles Journet, *The Meaning of Evil* (P. J. Kenedy & Sons, 1963); C. S. Lewis, *A Grief Observed* (Bantam Books, 1983) and *The Problem of Pain* (Touchstone Books, 1996); Jacques Maritain, "Blessed Are the Persecuted," in *The Range of Reason* (Scribner's, 1952); Columba Marmion, *Suffering with Christ* (Sands & Co., 1952); Émile Mersch, *The Whole Christ* (Dennis Dobson, 1962); and Jürgen Moltmann and Johannes B. Metz, *Meditations on the Passion* (Paulist Press, 1979).

R. S.

Index